Temporal Processes in Beethoven's Music

Temporal Processes in Beethoven's Music

David B. Greene

Wabash College
Crawfordsville, Indiana

GORDON AND BREACH SCIENCE PUBLISHERS

New York   London   Paris

Gordon and Breach, Science Publishers, Inc.
One Park Avenue
New York, NY 10016

Gordon and Breach Science Publishers Ltd.
42 William IV Street
London, WC2N 4DE

Gordon & Breach
58, rue Lhomond
75005 Paris

Library of Congress Cataloging in Publication Data

Greene, David B.
　　Temporal processes in Beethoven's music.

　　Includes index.
　　1. Beethoven, Ludwig van, 1770–1827 — Aesthetics.
2. Musical form.　I. Title.
ML410.B42G73　　　780′.92′4　　　81-2075
ISBN 0-677-05600-1　　　　　　　AACR2

Contents

Preface

MUSIC, LIKE TIME, seems to be better understood before we ask what it is. But it is hard not to ask. We go on thinking while we feel. Music amazes us, and the wonder we feel in its presence turns into wondering about the way it is important to us. Both kinds of wonder show our gratitude for the music, and the more grateful we are the more we want to wonder in a way that fits the music.

We also wonder about human existence. Philosophers like Kant, Husserl and Heidegger tell us that human consciousness is always, even necessarily, temporal: we always distinguish what is from that has been and from what is coming; we also synthesize past, present and future, for we are always recollecting and hoping at the same time that we are making an observation or a decision. If these philosophers are right, and if we are to deepen our understanding of human existence, we must think about the nature of the temporal process. We must recognize and perhaps modify our assumptions about continuity with the past and fulfillment in the future.

Everyone knows that music is temporal. Not everyone recognizes that different pieces are temporal in different ways, or that each piece puts together remembering and expecting in its own way, and so creates its own criteria of coherence, continuity and fulfillment.

Putting these questions and ruminations together leads to the following idea: music is important to us partly, perhaps even largely, because it offers us aural images of temporality. Sometimes confirming and sometimes challenging the way we have been distinguishing and synthesizing what is, what has been and what is coming, the temporal processes in music can lead us into a fresh awareness of the nature of change and continuity, or they may lead us to experience change and continuity in a new way.

The idea that music matters to us because its images of temporality matter to us is suggestive. It intimates that asking about the assumptions of change, continuity, coherence and fulfillment that are implicit in a piece may lead us to hear aspects of the piece we did not notice before. Our transaction with the music will be improved; it will matter even more. This book will test this suggestion by analyzing six of Beethoven's pieces. It will try to show that the impact of these movements on us deepens as we see them risking discontinuity while struggling toward a deeper kind of continuity, sometimes transforming our notion of fulfillment, sometimes leading us to accept ambiguity and incompleteness.

Most contemporary musicologists prefer not to use philosophical concepts, such as "temporal process", in analyzing music. They remember the nineteenth-century critics who applied philosophical categories in ways that were alien to the music, not really guided by the music and hence incapable of illumining it. Because every piece of music projects a temporal process, however, the use of this category does not have to be alien to the music. It ought to lead further into the music. It ought to be a means for making explicit what is implicitly present in the music.

Examining a piece's temporal process can also be a means for recognizing the suppositions that guide musicologists' analyses of the music. Like everyone else, a musicologist has basic beliefs — too basic to be easily stated — about the nature of movement, coherence and completion. Working from these assumptions, he or she develops metaphors like "line", "progression" and "texture" to describe different aspects of music and to identify various ways in which movement, coherence and completion — as he or she understands them — are achieved. When a piece seems unintelligible, the reason may be that its temporal process deviates too widely from the analyst's implicit beliefs about change and completion. When musicologists disagree, the reason may be that they are guided by different basic assumptions about what can count as continuity and fulfillment. Reflecting philosophically on temporality may be a way to specify the source of disagreement.

The idea that music matters to us because its images of temporality matter to us may suggest to philosophers that they may learn from music. Composers project their own understanding of the temporal process; they do not merely illustrate concepts that can just as well be stated verbally. If philosophers hear what the music offers, they can agree or disagree with it, build on it or reject it. Although insights into temporality offered in musical works cannot be exhaustively translated into verbal terms, one can point toward these aural images, and they can enrich philosophical descriptions of the temporal process.

If it is valid to think of music as projecting a temporal process, it may also be valid to think about the kinds of temporality implicitly presented by novels, poems, religious symbols, scientific models, and even paintings. Paying attention to temporal processes may enable us usefully to compare these varied forms of human expression — usefully because the comparisons may illumine each one and make it possible to identify lines of influence. Thinking about temporal processes may lead us to see that the areas separated by labels like "the arts", "religion", "science" and "philosophy" are not really separate after all. Although this book does not attempt a comprehensive study of temporal processes conveyed in all these different forms, it draws some comparison between pieces of music and the philosophies of Leibniz, Kant, Schelling, Hegel, Husserl and Heidegger.

For the reader's convenience, a large number of musical examples are reproduced in the book. Figures 1, 4, 13 and 16 were drawn by Richard R. Strawn. The excerpt from Bach's *St. Matthew Passion* uses the C.F. Peters edition. All the rest of the examples are taken from Belwin Mills editions and are reproduced with the publisher's authorization. In the case of the Beethoven sonatas, it might have been preferable to have used Bertha Wallner's critical edition, but permission for so many examples proved to be prohibitively expensive. The differences between the critical edition and the edition used have been carefully checked to make certain that none of the differences bear on the aspects of the music that are described in the text.

DAVID B. GREENE

Introduction:
Temporal Processes in Music

SEEING OURSELVES as human beings means seeing ourselves involved in a temporal process. In one way or another, we are always aware of a contrast between what is and what was and what will be. Generally we suppose that this contrast is, or ought to be, experienced by everyone in the same way; our sense of ourselves seems to suggest that the nature of the temporal process is simply given — fixed in the way things are — and we cannot imagine that others live in a temporal process that is really different from our own. Yet the difference between present, past and future and the nature of the movement from past to future is in fact variously experienced. Sometimes the difference is felt to be between what seems to be and what enduringly is. Sometimes it is between what seems to be and what can be. Sometimes it is between what is and what must be, or between what ought to have been and what might be. Some people experience change as an illusion and suppose that only some sort of underlying, unchanging qualities are real, while others feel that putative qualities or selves are illusory, and some people live in a temporality that combines these apparently contradictory experiences.

A great deal is at stake in the question, "What is my experience of the contrast between what is and what was and what will be, and what is the importance of this contrast," or, more briefly, "What is the nature of the temporal process?" For one thing, the answer to this question is so critical to one's self-understanding that people who live in sharply contrasting temporal processes can scarcely understand one another. To the extent that they suppose that there is only one possible temporal process — only one possible way of experiencing the contrast between what is and was and will be and only one kind

1

of importance that this contrast can have — and that it is simply given, they may not even realize that they do not understand each other, or if they do, they may not recognize the root of the problem.

For another thing, the kind of temporality one lives is very much the same as the way life itself feels. The texture and quality of life feels one way if what will be is what must be, if making plans means discovering one's destiny, if, as Mary Tyrone says in O'Neill's *Long Day's Journey into Night*, "The past is the future," so that to move into the future is only to feel the tightening grip of the past. The texture of experience is very different if one lives in a temporal process in which what will be is what may be (not what must be) and the future is to be created (not merely discovered) and the past is the context (not the generator) of the future.

And, finally, the question about the nature of the temporal process is important because its answer affects one's supposition about fulfillment. For example, some people suppose that the past and the present consist of tendencies and strivings that call into concrete reality a future that responds to them and fulfills their struggle. These people must somehow decide whether the future can indeed consist of climaxes and points of arrival that really embody that toward which the past and present are working. Or is there always something disappointing about the future, when it becomes the present, because some important promise is only partially fulfilled? Some people suppose that the future present inevitably and utterly fails to concretize the thrusts of the past's presents. This supposition leads to the further question, is perfect consummation even desirable; can a person live without some as yet unfulfilled goals? Is anything ever enough? And how is one to deal with less than complete fulfillment? By resigning oneself to disillusionment? By hoping for less? By retreating into some kind of non-temporal existence in which a deeper self does not participate in the temporal process, and is thus immune to its hopes, risks, despairs and joys? And how does one (or can one?) decide whether such a retreat is desirable?

Generally, we do not face these questions squarely, and the reason is that the temporal process itself is invisible. We habitually understand our experience in terms of its content, and are not explicitly aware of the temporal structure shaping that content. Nevertheless, we do deal with these questions in an oblique fashion through our religion, literature and science. For religious myths, literary symbols and scientific models implicitly assume and indirectly project various understandings of the temporal process while ostensibly dealing with other matters. When we let our experience be organized, however unselfconsciously, in accordance with a myth, symbol or model, we become infected with its view of temporality. To writers like Kant, Hegel, Husserl, Heidegger, Bergson, Poulet and McLuhan,[1] who have in their various ways tried to make these invisible structures at least conceptually visible, our debt is immense.

The burden of this introductory essay is to claim of music that it deals directly with the bundle of questions wrapped up in the term, "temporal process."[2] It does not merely assume an understanding of the temporal process while ostensibly dealing with other matters. For each sound in a piece is meaningful largely because of its relation to preceding and coming sounds,[3] and consequently a musical flow presents directly — far more directly than do myths, symbols and models — a particular understanding of temporality. Asking what that understanding is means inquiring about the piece's particular way of constrasting a present to a past and wondering about the kind of fulfillment that it sees as desirable and the extent to which it regards fulfillment as realizable.[4] When a piece feels important to us, the reason may be that its temporal process closely resembles our own, and if so, then thinking about its temporal process may make visible the hitherto invisible structure of our own experience and give us the opportunity to embrace or resist that piece's power to convince us that its temporality is the only one viable. Asking what image of temporality is projected by a piece that is important to another person or a different culture is a way into the other's self-understanding and enhances the possibility that, in spite of the fact that life feels quiet different to the other, we may begin to understand that person, culture or era. When a piece does not feel important to us, the reason may be that its temporal process contradicts our assumptions about temporality, and if so, we may want to set our assumptions aside provisionally and move into the temporality that the piece is proposing. Having done so, we may find that it makes more sense musically and its impact on us is enhanced. We may even find that we want to move more or less permanently into the temporality that it is suggesting. Or we may find that it contradicts too many significant aspects of our other experiences ever to feel important to us.

Although a piece's presentation of a view of temporality is direct, it is nevertheless metaphorical. As Nelson Goodman might say, it is figuratively an example of a temporal process.[5] Music provides literal samples of various kinds of sounds (trumpet sounds, violin sounds, and so forth), and because they are temporally deployed — they are heard successively and not all at once — music provides literal examples of repetition and of changes of timbre, pitch, duration and amplitude. But these sounds, repetitions and changes become music only when they are heard as projecting things like progression, closure, climax and resolution. Of these aspects music provides metaphorical, not literal, samples. (A literal sample of closure, for instance, would be a parliamentary body taking up an issue, deciding it by taking a vote, and adjourning.) It is aspects like progression and closure, which music exemplifies figuratively, and not aspects like sound, repetition and change as such, which music exemplifies literally, that are critical to a piece's presentation of a temporal process. Consequently, one must say that it offers a metaphor for, or an aural image of, a temporal process, and not a literal instance of it.

Recognizing that a piece metaphorically presents a temporal process implies that becoming aware of its way of relating past, present and future is far more like responding to metaphors in poetry than like analyzing the acoustics of sound.[6] This fact does not distinguish the study of temporality in music from other kinds of musical analysis: whenever analysts talk about harmonic progressions or musical shape they are trying to identify aspects of which the music provides metaphorical and not literal samples. For instance, analysts say things like, "This chord goes to that chord"; what is literally true is that the first is heard, then the second, but in saying that the first "goes to" the second, analysts are suggesting that the succession is a metaphor for motion, and they usually go on to suggest the kind of motion that is figuratively exemplified. For another instance, analysts sometimes say that a passage is "unstable," suggesting it has aspects in common with those of a wobbly chair. The former is a metaphorical example of instability, just as the latter is a literal example.

Any analysis of music, and especially one analyzing its temporal process, needs to pay attention to the nature of metaphors so that it will claim the appropriate kind of validity for its results.[7] Someone who does not hear a set of sounds as a metaphor for, say, closure, is likely to suspect that those who do are importing their own experiences into the music. Although it is not unusual for insensitive listeners to impose their own ideas on the music, it is important to insist that metaphors are not necessarily idiosyncratic, nor are they necessarily false just because they are not literally true. One can say that "time is a beggar," and recognize that, while the statement is not literally true, time is indeed a figurative example of a beggar. Insight is required to recognize the aspects of time and of beggars such that one is metaphorically an instance of the other.[8] Insight is very different from imposition, though the person who cannot see the metaphor also cannot see the difference. Both a range of experience and also reflection on experience are necessary prerequisites to insight, and one whom the insight eludes is likely to suspect that the metaphor either barely touches or else clumsily tramples on the musical experience.

Identifying that of which a certain aspect of a piece of music is figuratively a sample is complicated by the fact that the metaphorical relation also works the other way around. A particular passage of music has a quality that is radically peculiar to it, and applying a term like "climax" to it means that this concept is a metaphor for this absolutely unique quality. The concept is figuratively an instance of that which is literally a class of one. The passage is not merely an instance, figurative or literal, of a climax; it is its particular self, and the concept of "climax" is offered to illumine its particular quality.

But if the concept illumines the particularity, the passage must also illumine the concept, just as an aspect of "beggar" as well as of "time" is uncovered when we see that "time is a beggar." An aspect of "climax" is uncovered when we see that it appropriately applies to a particular passage of music. Music analysts and critics are thus constantly working in two directions, trying to choose words that will both reveal how they hear the music (finding metaphors for the music) and also show how the music organizes or alters or bears on other experiences (identifying that for which the music is a metaphor).

Everyone recognizes that it is impossible to provide recipes whereby a composer may always write a successful passage. It is also impossible to specify procedures that will guarantee that critics will have so paid attention to the specific quality both of the music and of non-musical experience that the metaphors they create to link the two will be helpful, revealing and compelling to their readers. When a metaphor fails, it may be obscure either because the critic tried to be profound but has not yet wrested from the music or the other experiences their secret or because the readers have not had the pertinent musical or concrete experiences. Or it may fail by being obvious, a cliche that skims the surface of one or the other. Every metaphor risks failure; there can be no guarantees that it is neither obscure nor obvious. The risk of failure is somewhat mitigated by the fact that an obscure metaphor may nevertheless be suggestive and an obvious one felicitous.

Even listeners who habitually resist applying their own or other's metaphors to music recognize that music is not merely entertaining, but that it has something to do with the rest of life. They do not deny that music affects our thinking and feeling, but they doubt that the effect can be specified. Recognizing that what a critic does is not to provide literal descriptions but to build metaphors undercuts their denial to some extent, although, of course, only the compelling metaphor really reverses their attitude. If it is the case, as has been suggested above, that musical pieces directly present images of temporal processes and that one's sense of the temporal process in which one is involved is directly implicated in one's sense of human experience at its most fundamental level, then it may also be the case that compelling metaphors for a piece can be generated by asking what temporal process it presupposes and projects. It may be, in other words, that metaphors related to the temporal process both go to the heart of music and also uncover the way music affects our thinking and feeling.

Each piece has its own temporal process, and so one should talk about the temporal process it presents, not about the temporal process in music generally. Most of this book is devoted to the temporal processes in particular movements by Ludwig van Beethoven. Works by Beethoven have been chosen because they feel important to many of us, and if the approach to music analysis proposed here is valid, it must be able to enhance their impact and deepen our understanding of their importance to us. Moreover, Beethoven's temporal processes are more diverse than those of most other composers, including the great ones. In one way or another the temporality projected by each of the selected movements is highly unusual. Differing from one another, they also diverge from and challenge — at the same time that they reflect — assumptions about temporality and human experience that have prevailed in Western thinking for the last two centuries.

While it is meaningless to ask what is the temporal process in music generally, it is nevertheless true that pieces composed by the same person or cast in the same form or written in the same style period have significant analogies with one another. Analyzing pieces that may be grouped together because of their analogies can pave the way to describing the Beethoven movements: the study of such pieces illustrates what is involved in the question, "How is the contrast between what is, what has been and what is coming understood in a particular piece of music?" and it furnishes examples of temporal processes to which Beethoven's processes can be contrasted. For these two reasons, the rest of this introduction will offer some generalizations about temporality in J.S. Bach's music, in Classic sonata-allegro movements and in Romantic music.

1. *Temporality in Bach's Music*

Bach's music is an aural image of Newtonian time. In the Newtonian world-view, the totality of material entities constitutes a universe in the sense that they all operate according to the same laws which exhaustively explain their behavior. The location, mass and velocity of every entity at any given time is a function of the location, mass and velocity of all entities at the previous instant of time. If one knows the laws of motion, as Isaac Newton believed he did, and if one knew the location, mass and velocity of all particles at any one time, as Newton did not believe he did, then one could move either forward or backward in time and describe definitively these parameters at all other times. Although things may happen that are not predicted, nothing that is in principle unpredictable, if one had sufficient data, can happen. The pattern of change is fixed and constant.

The basic premise of seventeenth- and eighteenth-century rationalism is that all change, including human behavior and feeling, operates by principles analogous to those governing Newton's material universe. Leibniz's thinking, for example, is informed by the supposition that everything develops by analogy to the way a mathematical or logical system unfolds. Everything in the realm of human nature is as predictable as planetary motion. For rationalists like Alexander Pope, the very expression "human nature" suggests that even the human soul has a nature and can be understood within a system of thought comprehending both material and spiritual nature. If rationalists are faithful to their premises, they believe that history is completely determined and that human behavior is in principle predictable. Thorough-going rationalism implies that the future of individuals and society is implicit in the present, and one could know the future if one knew the laws governing human nature and had sufficient data about the present.

In a consistently Newtonian world-view, then, the future, both human and material, would be the unfolding of a necessity. The future would consist of events that, given the present, could not fail to happen. Bach's inventions, sonata movements, fugues, concerto movements, arias and choruses are the aural image of such an unfolding necessity.[9] A strong caesura characterizes the endings of these movements; they run a course, and at the final cadence the listener is satisfied that the course is completely finished. Along the way, the music has been dominated, and thus unified, by one or two motifs. These melodic or rhythmic fragments are stated in various voices, beginning on various pitches, and are combined in various ways. By the end, all the possible ways of presenting and combining the motifs seem to have been exploited, so the motivic play contributes to the sense of completeness as well as of unity. During the course of the piece, the motivic play does not seem capricious, and the reason it does not has to do with the bass line and the harmonic progressions. The bass line moves so constantly and steadily that it articulates a motor rhythm on which the motivic play rides. The motor rhythm is so persistent that it seems inexorable and lends a quality of inexorableness to the motivic play as well: the particular ways a motif is restated and combined with itself seem as inevitable as though they were derived exclusively from the motif's own features.

The bass line also implies a series of harmonies that do not merely succeed one another, but also seem to progress from one to the next. The harmonic march cooperates with the constant movement of the bass to generate the sense of inevitable forward motion. The harmonic progressions determine goals, and when the motivic play arrives at these goals, it comes to a momentary rest. The choice of the temporary tonal centers articulated by these cadences seems no more capricious than the motivic play, for the temporary tonics invariably emphasize the important notes of the home-key scale, the longer the movement, the more of these tones being stressed. In a short minor-key movement, the pitches emphasized by the cadences are usually the tonic, the relative major and the dominant, in that order. In the D Minor Two-part Invention, for example, they are D, F and A — the three pitches of the triad built on the movement's tonic. The cadences of a short major-key movement typically emphasize the tonic, the dominant and the relative minor — C, G and A in the C Major Two-part Invention. The end of the movement usually goes into the subdominant long enough to balance the dominant, so that the tonic is circled by emphasized pitches a fifth above and a fifth below itself.

When it is over, the movement has become a picture of orderliness. Although the rhythm, harmony and motivic play have influenced one another profoundly but have not literally determined each other, everything that has happened seems to have happened for a completely sufficient reason. The satisfaction most listeners feel at the close comes from their sense that everything that has happened (such as stating the motif in F, in the D-Minor Invention) has not happened by accident or caprice, but had to happen, and that everything that needed to happen has in fact taken place. This reasonableness is not, however, completely apparent before the end of the movement. Like a complex but smoothly running machine, there are gears within gears, and as one is moving through the piece one cannot be sure at first whether an event is happening on a larger or smaller gear. Consequently, the experience of listening to this music involves considerable uncertainty, but the unity of the motivic play convinces one that the laws whose hidden operation regulates the putative uncertainties will be revealed by the end of the movement, and the reason for the temporarily unexpected events will become palpable. As in Newton's universe, unpredicted events are surprising only because one does not yet have sufficient data or understand sufficiently well the laws of motion.

FIGURE 1

J.S. Bach, Fugue in G Minor for Organ, BWV 542

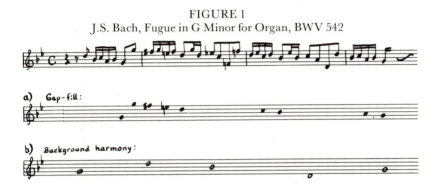

The subject in Bach's G Minor Fugue (BWV 542) is a handy example because what happens in miniature here also happens on a larger scale in other pieces. Early on, the fugue subject skips from G to G an octave higher, leading the listener to expect the gap to be filled by a stepwise return to the lower G (Figure 1). Leonard Meyer calls attention to the fact that, on the third beat of the second measure, this expectation is temporarily frustrated.[10] Looking at Figure 1a, one sees how much longer the subject takes for the step from D to C than for any other step in the gap-fill. By the end of the subject, this deviation from what is expected, as well as other, briefer ones, makes the final arrival at the lower G more satisfying than would a direct, uninhibited descent. What Meyer does not mention, but is even more important to the picture of orderliness drawn by the fugue subject, is the fact that the deviations serve a purpose beyond simply delaying the arrival on G: The descent from D to C takes longer than other steps in the gap-fill because B-flat is, during this step, made into a temporary tonic. This deviation thereby gives B-flat an emphasis that is as strong as the emphases on G and D in the background harmony (Figure 1b). These three pitches together constitute the G minor triad, which is also articulated by the first six notes (and the last six, which are identical to the first six) of the subject. Thus, the background harmony as well as the opening and closing six notes of the subject is a horizontal version of the vertical chord that is the backbone of the whole movement. The particular way that Bach deviates from what is expected, and not the sheer fact of deviation, contributes to the image of temporarily unexpected events becoming reasonable. Departing from the path of least resistance does not happen for the sheer fun of stating the motif an extra time nor simply for the sake of postponing an arrival and intensifying the affect. Rather the deviation is guided by and thus exhibits the operation of a higher-level principle. Because the principle determines the course of the motivic play, which in turn unifies the three measures, the fugue subject can serve as a metaphor for the unfolding of a necessity.

Hearing a performance of Bach's music chugging along to a conclusion that will feel inevitable is, then, like the process of gaining a perspective from which change is experienced not as vicissitude or as the result of making a decision but as patterned movement. Although different performances of the same piece may project somewhat different patterns, each performance is a process in which there is change, but the change is ordered, and the principle of the order is fixed and unchanging. If the music leads to a perspective from which one recognizes unchanging order and if the contrast of present, past and future necessarily presupposes change, then this perspective stands outside the temporal process. The experience of listening to a Bach movement is the experience of moving through a temporal process to that which endures non-temporally.

Bach's recitatives, fantasias and toccatas, because of their lack of motivic unity, their harmonic capriciousness and their rhythmic nervousness, do not end with a strong closure. They invariably open into a movement that does — an aria or a fugue (exceptions to this generalization are apparent, not real; for example, the G Major Fantasia, BWV 572, contains its orderly movement as its center section, and the closing section simply prolongs the G major cadence).

In Bach's passions, the recitatives narrate the biblical account of Jesus's arrest, trial and death, and each aria meditates on some aspect of the narration. The contours of the evangelist's line and the harmonic progressions are to a certain extent suggested by the words of the text, and their lack of higher-level coherence mirrors the apparent vicissitudes and unpredictability of real-life history. The arias' texts invite listeners to identify themselves with Jesus or his disciples or with the ideal worshiper and to sink down into some point in that history. For a time, they leave the narrative sequence. The arias' musical process, sketched above, of leading the listener through a temporal process to a non-temporal, ahistorical position not only interrupts history (in its retold form) but also leaves history. The arias invite the listener to participate in Jesus's history not by doing what he did or by furthering his cause but by grasping the meaning of the events of his life and moving to an ahistorical position. Authentic religious experience, the passions suggest, consists of consummating concrete historical experiences in the same way that the arias consummate the recitatives and satisfy their restless searching, namely by bouncing off history into a place where change ceases because one sees the orderliness of the change, and the pattern of change does not change at all.

The relationship between the fantasias and toccatas to their fugues is analogous to that of the recitatives to their arias. The fantasias and toccatas are, of course, wordless abstractions from particular concrete experiences. Yet their rhapsodic meanderings bespeak the same restlessness as the recitatives in the passions (and the cantatas, too), and lead into the fugue's picture of order. The toccatas mirror the uncertainties of life, the fugues mirror the unchanging order that regulates apparent lawlessness, and the relationship between the two — that is, the way the first defines the register, tonality and timbre in which the second will happen and unleashes the energies which the second will organize — mirrors the way the vagaries of concrete experience create a felt need for a perspective from which the randomness of experience can be recognized as apparent, not real.

Each of Bach's movements that ends with strong closure is unified by a motif that is distinctive to that movement. This individuality, however, is subordinate to the order that the rhythm and harmony create, just as in Newton's universe the particular uniqueness of each entity (and even of each person) is subordinated to the laws common to the behaviour of all entities.

The *da capo* arias do not easily fit this generalization, because in them the contrast between the motif controlling the first and third sections and the motif controlling the middle section is often strong enough to suggest that the distinctiveness of the motifs is upheld as an important musical dynamic. The motif of each section evokes a picture, and the juxtaposition of the two pictures is more or less violent and more or less dramatic. The drama is, however, more pictorial than musical because there is little or no musical thrust across the end of the first to the beginning of the second section. For by the end of the first section the rhythmic energy has been completely or almost completely spent, the motor rhythm comes to rest, and, unlike the recitative, the section ends with strong closure. (Figure 2, bar 29, is an example.) Thus the second section cannot be said to have been generated by the first. Like the first section, the second ends with a cessation of motor rhythm and a strong closure (Figure 2, bar 45). In short, where the motor rhythm and purposive harmonic march press forward in their inexorable way, there is no change (within each section, as within a fugue, the motif is constant), and change happens (a new motif appears) only after the motor rhythm has stopped. It is as though time began anew with the middle, contrasting section. A second orderliness is offered.

Because of the rupture in the temporal flow at the beginning of the middle section, this moment sounds anything but inevitable. But precisely the arbitrariness of the event and the contrast of its picture to the first section's picture creates a tension which the repeat of the opening section resolves. In other words, because of the contrast of the first to the middle section, the third section begins with a strong sense of return. The beginning of the *da capo*, in spite of the break in the flow, is as predictable as the beginning of the second section seems arbitrary. And the return retrospectively gives the departure a purpose — namely, to set up the conditions making possible the satisfying feeling that the return arouses.

This way of describing the return makes it seem that the resolution is in fact a rejection; restating the first picture without the slightest alteration suggests that the contrasting section is completely irrelevant to the orderly picture drawn in the first section and that the second orderliness is offered for the sole purpose of being discarded.

This inference is incorrect, however, because it overlooks the fact that the third section affects the listener differently from the first section precisely because the contrasting section illumines the character of the returning music. The contrast heightens the listener's awareness and appreciation of the distinctive character peculiar to the first section's music. Becoming aware of what a thing is different from generally sharpens one's awareness of the first thing. Contrast fails to serve such a function when the differences are too subtle or too gross. One learns little about a particular orange by comparing it to a second fruit that has no conspicuous differences (and one would say, presumably, that the second fruit is another orange). One's appreciation of an orange's unique quality can be heightened by comparing it to a grapefruit, but very little by comparing it to an elephant and even less by comparing it to an electron, unless one can see significant resemblances in addition to the obvious contrasts. It is critical to the *da capo* process that the contrasts are not gross: the middle section has generally the same range, meter, tempo and instrumentation as the first section. Contrasts as violent as those in "Es ist vollbracht" from the *St. John passion* are rare. Moreover, the contrasting section is always harmonically coordinated with the opening section. It is invariably centered on one of the important notes of the first's scale, usually the relative minor or the relative major. In other words, the two sections are similar enough that their differences are mutually illuminating.

But although the three sections of the *da capo* aria are relevant to one another and by the end of the middle section the return to the music of the first section seems inevitable, the aria as a whole does not seem to project the image of a temporal process in which the future is totally predictable. There are events within a fugue or an aria's first section that are not, in fact, determined, but the motor rhythm, tight harmonic progressions and motivic unity mask the lack of total determination. In the *da capo* aria, the rupture in the motor rhythm and the motivic contrasts inject a measure of randomness into the picture. This randomness, unlike that in a recitative (or prelude) followed by an aria (or fugue), persists.

The rupture in the musical flow is, of course, even more complete between the various arias and choruses of a cantata, oratorio or mass and between the individual movements of a suite or sonata. These arias or movements are harmonically coordinated, though the harmonic relations are sometimes looser than those between the sections of a *da capo* aria. Sometimes an alternation of slow and fast tempi or of sad and happy moods creates a pattern. One senses, however, far less inevitability in moving from one movement to the next than in moving through a single movement.

The middle section of a *da capo* aria is a middle section not only in the sense that it falls between two other sections but also in the sense that its contours are such that it would sound wrong if it were an opening or a closing section. Its elaboration is generally not quite sufficient to sound conclusive at its end. Like an aria following a recitative or a fugue following a prelude, it seems to depend on the first section to have defined the range, timbre and tonality it uses, for it cannot both define these parameters and also move within them. And to some extent, it seems to require a contrast — namely, that to the opening section — to sound meaningful, for its own statement is not sufficiently definite to stand on its own.

Similarly, some of the opening movements in the cantatas seem particularly appropriate in their position, and the chorales or choruses at the end seem especially conclusive summaries of the work as a whole. The fast gigues make rousing endings to the suites and

FIGURE 2
"Blute nur", soprano aria from Bach, *St. Matthew Passion*. Reproduced by kind permission of Peters Edition, London, Frankfurt and New York

partitas in which they occur. In many cases one feels that the inner movements would be less effective if they had been in either the beginning or the ending position. But Bach's own practice erodes one's confidence in judgments of this sort: Who, on hearing the "Gratias agimus tibi" within the Gloria of the B Minor Mass would guess that this music, with no changes at all, could be used as effectively as it is to end the Mass with the text, "dona nobis pacem"?

In short, some aspects of the various movements in cantatas, sonatas, and suites articulate a pattern that orders the movements into a whole. But the picture of orderliness is far sketchier and the sense of inevitability is far weaker in the process of moving from one movement to the next than in moving through a single movement. This observation underscores the importance of the basso continuo with its motor rhythm and harmonic purposiveness in creating the sense of inevitability that characterizes the end of each movement. Where the motor rhythm stops, the sense of inevitability dims. It dims more as one goes from one movement to the next in a cantata or suite than as one goes from one section to the next in a *da capo* aria.

In the Newtonian world-view, the idea that the future is the unfolding of a necessity presupposes that one knows or can know the unchanging laws of motion and the location and velocity of all particles of matter at some given moment. A fugue, a chorus or a sonata movement is an image of this way of experiencing the contrast between the present and the future. The future is knowable in principle, yet unknown in fact if one believes that there are laws of motion but that one does not yet know them or if one does not know all the parameters of the present. The future is determined, but because one does not know the actual content that is determined, it seems somewhat random as it happens. The less one's notions approximate reality, the greater the apparent randomness. One's confidence that the randomness is only apparent is based on an idea, not an observation. The idea qualifies experience as much as observation, for apparently random events feel one way if one believes that they are in fact random and quite a different way if one believes that there are principles of determination and that they are discoverable. A *da capo* aria, a cantata or a suite is an image of the latter way of experiencing the contrast between the present and the future. The degree of apparent randomness is much less in the single aria than in the cantata as a whole. Moving through the sections of an aria is the image of moving into a future that is (one believes) totally determined but that seems nearly, and not completely, inevitable because one's notion of the laws of motion and of the present location and velocity of particles closely approximates reality.

Moving through the movements of a cantata or suite is the image of moving into a future which seems less inevitable and in which events appear more random because the approximation is less good, even though again, they are believed to be totally determined. The individual fugue or chorus or suite movement resembles the eighteenth-century rationalists' ideal of the temporal process — the way the contrast between present and future ought to be, and someday will be, experienced — while the *da capo* arias and the cantatas, sonatas and suites (as whole works) resemble their actual experience of temporality.

Both the ideal and the actual experience of the rationalists presuppose that the laws of motion are knowable in principle and that the present can be known in enough detail to permit one to predict the future. If one denies either of these premises, then the future is unknowable in principle. Events will seem random, and while one believes that the randomness is apparent rather than real, one despairs of ever experiencing anything but randomness. No Baroque pieces offer an image of this way of experiencing the contrast between the present and the future, for its assumptions flatly contradict the most basic premise of rationalism — that the world is rational and that the human mind can grasp the world's rationality.

2. *Temporality in Sonata-Allegro Form in the High Classic Period*

By the end of the eighteenth century, the French Revolution and the ideas of liberty, equality and fraternity which it sought to embody were reshaping social and political structures in some countries and challenging the status quo everywhere in Europe. In talking about these changes, people generally used a vocabulary derived from Newtonian thinking, for by then it controlled common sense and its language. So they saw the changes as an orderly process working linearly toward goals that were foreordained in the sense of being caused and determined by the nature of things. Revolution meant moving to the way society ought to be. Changes were the unfolding of a necessity. Any other kind of change involved leaving the temporal process.[11]

There were some, however, who sensed a discrepancy between the way social change felt and the way it was generally talked about. Immanuel Kant, in his *Critique of Pure Reason* (1781) showed that the human mind always imposed its categories of time and space on natural objects, and while things-in-themselves did not exist in time and space their appearances to the mind invariably did. Kant drew a sharp line between natural objects and entities like free human will and God that were not accessible to sensible intuition. Such entities may and even must be postulated, but they cannot be known. Since one may not assume that their temporality — that is, the way they experience and participate in a contrast between past, present and future — is the same as the temporality with which natural objects appear to us, one could not correctly know, Kant believes, human and divine temporality. G.W.F. Hegel (1770–1831) developed the category of history as a means of providing precisely what Kant believed could not be done. The thrust of Hegel's lectures on the Philosophy of History (1822–25) was to create a conceptuality in which changes like the eighteenth-century upheavals could be understood as brought about by people creating history, a process not at all analogous to the mechanical operation of cause and effect in nature. History was completely rational, but the criteria of its rationality were not the same as those of the natural world.[12]

In music, sonata-allegro form offered an image of the temporal process that, like Hegel's, was an alternative to the Newtonian way of understanding change.[13] Composers of instrumental chamber music developed what has come to be called sonata-allegro form during the 1770s. F.J. Haydn and W.A. Mozart perfected the form during the 1780s, and by the early 1790s, pieces in the form were very popular among the increasing numbers of middle-class amateur musicians in cities like Vienna, Leipzig, Paris and London. One reason for its popularity may be that, concurrently with the social changes in Europe, sonata-allegro form had developed a non-verbal way of thinking about change in the temporal process that corresponded more closely to the way change was being experienced than did Newtonian language.

To say that Hegel and sonata-allegro form rejected Newtonian temporality is not to say that either one presented change as apocalyptic. Where one fears or hopes that change is apocalyptic, the past is seen to have been completely repudiated and the future is regarded as a radically new beginning, utterly cut off from the past. The very popularity of sonata-allegro form suggests that most middle-class people did not feel they were undergoing an apocalyse.

In the image of temporality projected by sonata-allegro form, the present calls a future into being. This future is genuinely responsive to the past (unlike the future in apocalyptic temporality). Yet it also feels like a fresh occurrence, an eventful occurrence, and not one that happens by logical or mechanical necessity (unlike the future in Newtonian temporality).[14]

The term "eventful occurrence" is being used here in a special sense that needs to be clarified. We may call an occurrence "eventful" if we can suppose that it might not have happened and if its happening injects into history some genuinely new dynamic. The thrust of Newtonian temporality, by contrast, is to see all occurrences as uneventful — as occurrences that cannot *not* happen. Each particular event, in the Newtonian world-view, is an instance of the operation of a universal law. The concept of an eventful occurrence stresses the particularity of an event and not the general principle which, according to the Newtonian, it exemplifies. Although the eventful occurrence is analogous to other events — more closely analogous to some than to others — it is primarily itself and not simply an example of a class.

In order to suppose that an occurrence might not have happened it is necessary to suppose that the occurrence took the shape it did because people made decisions that they might not have made. In other words, the notion of an eventful occurrence presupposes that decisions are decisive: had a decision been different, the occurrence would have been different. This presupposition implies that when a person decides to do something, only his or her deciding it accounts, in the end, for it being done. Biological and social forces provide the context in which the decision is made, but if these are regarded as complete causes of the occurrence, the word "decision" ceases to be appropriate. Where "decision" is a meaningful word, one cannot know what a person will decide to do, no matter how many data or how many "laws of human nature" one knows. On the basis of prior experience, one may guess what another will do, and the guesses may usually be correct. In order that a decision be decisive and an occurrence eventful, it need not be surprising. Indeed, for a person to recognize that another person's decision is appropriate to its context, it must be possible for the former to imagine himself making the same decision if he were in the other's situation. Recognizing that a particular event is genuinely responsive to its particular past entails recognizing a kind of universality, but a kind very different from that which the rationalists presupposed and sought to make explicit.

It is impossible to imagine evidence that would compel a Newtonian to see decisions, understood in this way, as possible. No empirical evidence could disprove the supposition that biological and social forces exhaustively account for what get called "decisions". The point of invoking the term here is not to adjudicate that issue, but simply to set up the term as a metaphor for the kind of contrast between present, past and future that is projected by pieces in sonata-allegro form.

Pieces said to be in this form vary significantly from one another, but all of them involve the interaction of two elements: balance and forward thrust. Both elements pervade every level of sonata structure. The most obvious and perhaps the most important example is the paired phrases which occur in literally every Classic sonata.[15] Two phrases may be said to be paired if the second ends more stably than the first such that the ending of the second is heard as closing both of them. In other words, the first phrase is closed with a cadence (otherwise, it would not yet be a completed phrase), but along with this closure are elements of forward motion that carry across the cadence, linking the first phrase to the second. The first phrase is "anacrustic" — it metaphorically exemplifies a process that is literally exemplified by an unaccented syllable in poetry leading into the first accented syllable — and the second is "thetic" — it metaphorically exemplifies something that is prepared by and led into by something else. Because the first phrase ends with a cadence, it is distinct from the second at the same time that its anacrustic quality links it to the thetic gesture. As two distinct gestures, they balance one another, even if the second is somewhat longer than the first. At their end, the pair is not only closed but also thrusts forward *as a pair*. It is the pair (and not just the second phrase) that pushes into the next section of the music. In Baroque music, it is the motor rhythm, independent of the phrase structure, that keeps the music going.

Frequently, each phrase consists of two four-bar subphrases (or, more precisely, two subphrases each with four downbeats; a subphrase may be a beat or two longer than four measures if its first downbeat is preceded by an upbeat, and a subphrase may be a beat or two less than four measures if the next subphrase or section begins with an upbeat). These subphrases form a lower-level pair with each other exactly as the phrases form a higher-level pair. Also frequently, each subphrase is articulated in its middle so that one hears it as two downbeats plus two more. These articulations are not made by cadences, but they do exemplify the element of balance in the piece and show how even the smallest details feature it.

Figure 3 quotes the beginning of Mozart's "Eine kleine Nachtmusik," K. 525, in order to illustrate these aspects of paired phrases. The first phrase (bars 1–10) ends on the melodically unstable D, so that this phrase forms a pair with bars 11–18. The first phrase consists of a pair of subphrases (bars 1–4 and 5–10). The harmonic mobility characterizing the end of the first subphrase accounts for the forward thrust that links it to the second subphrase. A sequence

FIGURE 3

W.A. Mozart, Serenade in G for Strings, K. 525 ("Eine kleine Nachtmusik"), first movement

// = divisions within subphrases

‐ ‐ ‐ ‐ ⌐ = extension beyond the length of subphrase to which it is paired

tacked on to the end of the second subphrase extends it beyond the length of its pair. Almost every sonata-allegro movement has at least one example of such an expansion. The extension in bars 9–10 of "Eine kleine Nachtmusik" is needed to carry the melody from the stable G of bar 9 to the unstable D of bar 10; by landing first on G, the subphrase neatly forms a pair with bars 1–4; by moving on to D, the phrase as a whole (i.e. bars 1–10) thrusts forward, forming a pair with the second phrase (bars 11–18). Like the first, this second phrase consists of two subphrases. They form a pair because the first ends (bar 14) on a tone of melodic instability (B instead of the tonic, G). These subphrases are internally divided in an unusual way: the internal subdivisions fall after one measure (i.e. between 11 and 12 and between 15 and 16) instead of in the middle of the subphrases.

Paired phrases are essential to "Eine kleine Nachtmusik" and to Classical sonata-allegro movements in general. In order to make this point, Figure 4 shows how altering a very few notes can destroy the phrase pairings and totally change the character of Mozart's music. The phrases and subphrases have been made to end without any forward movement, so that one hears a series of four juxtaposed phrases, but no pairings. Because the phrases do not form groups, none of them can be said to balance another. None of them exemplifies a preparation for a balancing phrase, and none of them exemplifies the arrival of that which has been prepared. At the end of Figure 4, there is no tension that would justify continuing the piece.

FIGURE 4

In "Eine kleine Nachtmusik," as in sonata-allegro movements generally, the paired phrases with their internal, balancing divisions make a tight structure: the extent and depth of palpable organization work against a fluent musical sweep. The very tautness generates forward thrust into a looser, more flowing section.[16] Such a section invariably comes, and it usually comes immediately after the paired phrases. Because of the forward motion created in the paired phases, the fluent section forms a pair with them. In descriptions of music in sonata form, the term, "first theme," is often used to refer to the first set of paired phrases. The first flowing section is generally called the bridge because either harmonically or melodically or both it provides a transition to a second set of paired phrases. This second pair, usually called the second theme, is invariably in a different key from the first theme. It is always followed by a second fluent section, the exposition closing, with which it usually forms a pair. Because the second theme is generally stabler than the first theme[17] and because the first theme plus bridge generally begins in one key and ends in the new key, and is thus harmonically mobile, while the exposition closing usually ends in the key of the second theme, the first pair of sections generally forms a pair with the second pair of sections. As a pair of pairs, these four sections constitute a whole that is called the exposition.

The exposition is repeated. Ending in the new key, the first statement lacks harmonic closure, and this harmonic mobility provides the thrust that links the exposition as a whole with its repetition. The development section follows, and its looser organization, its less predictable harmonic and rhythmic contours and especially its ending (the "retransition"), dwelling for several measures on a single harmony and motif, make it as a whole form a pair with the recapitulation as a whole. This last section generally consists of a restatement of the first theme, the bridge (altered so that a new key is not established), the second theme (stated this time in the main key) the closing and sometimes a coda.

The elements of forward motion from the first member of a pair to the second (on whatever level) evoke the image of present events conjuring up a future as a metaphor for the process exemplified by the pairs. Listeners find themselves in a temporal process in which the things that are happening call forth new events. Hearing the forward thrust generated by bars 1–10 of "Eine kleine Nachtmusik" is like expecting fulfillment and looking toward completion. When the paired phrase begins in bar 11, the listener hears the arrival of the expected event. The summoned future takes shape and happens. Fulfillment is a public event.

It is important that these arrivals are not merely climactic points, although they begin that way, but that it is a whole phrase or section that responds to the summoning past, just as it is a whole phrase or section that summons a future, and not simply a motor rhythm or a single harmonic progression. Because the answer is a balancing phrase of section, and not a timeless point, the evoked future takes place in the same temporal process as that which evokes it. What the past calls into being actually comes into being. Not an infinitely short moment, it occupies some time and can be said to "happen." Fulfillment happens within the temporal process, not at some atemporal, timeless point.

The elements of balance and the fact that the paired groups are separated by an articulating cadence evoke the metaphor of a deciding agent. Essential to the Classic sonata-allegro process is the fact that arrival does not occur within the same phrase, but is separated by an articulating cadence from the past that evoked it. While the forward thrust to the arrival gives the sense of continuity within the temporal process, the fact that the arrival is a balancing phrase and so has its own beginning gives the sense of genuine change. Because of the dividing cadence, the balancing phrase or section seems fresh even if it begins with music that is exactly the same as that with which the other begins or ends. The arrival resembles an event that must be explained by both the past preparing it and by the unpredictable decision that severs the event from the past so that the future is not a merely mechanical continuation or repetition of the past.

This decision presupposes a deciding self that can take responsibility for its actions. Because the musical event does not exemplify metaphorically the operation of general laws, yet seems intelligible, the process it exemplifies seems in some sense to entail a rational subject. To assert that there is a relationship between the Classical musical event and a free self does not necessarily imply that the motif or theme is a metaphor for the presupposed self, nor that the motif or theme suggests what the self is like, nor that the transformations of the theme represent what the self undergoes.[18] Rather the process of a phrase or a section forming a pair with the phrase or section from which it is separated yet forward to which it presses is an image of the process in which the self makes a decision and actualizes itself through the event which that decision shapes.[19] The music does not illumine what this presupposed agent is before it makes a decision. Evidently it is atemporal (like the transcendental self in Kant's philosophy[20]) and while it is in some sense real it does not become a concrete actuality (like the empirical self in Kant) until it makes a decision and enacts itself temporally. As a summoned future takes shape and happens publicly, the self also becomes actual. To the extent that the arrival of the expected event really does fulfill its past, the self is also fully actual.

Events that respond to their past would not imply decisions were not some of them surprising in some way. Modern taste prefers those sonata-allegro movements whose surprises are profound and striking without being arbitrary. But even in compositions now judged to be second rate, the responding event takes its own turns, sometimes, for example, introducing internal subphrases or going beyond the length of the phrase to which it is paired. The listener feels both that the future summoned by the past has happened and that, far from a necessity unfolding, something has happened that did not have to happen. An eventful occurrence has taken place. In the second-rate works, the eventful occurrence is not very surprising. Their paired groups resemble processes in which one decides to perpetuate a routine and extend the status quo with| minimal alterations. But even a decision to follow routine patterns is a decision and not a matter of mechanical necessity. Where the eventful occurrence is more surprising as well as decisive, the music can serve as a more appropriate metaphor for the significant social upheavals that we call "revolutions."

Paired groups also resemble the process in which a responding event is fresh and a deciding self is involved by the way that as a pair they thrust forward into the next passage. A fresh response is fresh in that it introduces unpredictable elements, and these in their turn evoke another future. At bar 18 in "Eine kleine Nachtmusik," listeners feel a strong push into the next section (as they do not in bar 18 of Figure 4). Bars 11–18 both respond to bars 1–10 and at the same time work with bars 1–10 to evoke the subsequent event.

The process of a phrase thrusting forward to a balancing phase and then the pair generating a section that forms a pair with it, and so on, would become mechanical and even predictable were it not that the various pairings in any particular sonata-allegro movement are by no means equally strong. A number of different techniques give rise to forward thrust: sometimes the harmony, sometimes skips or repetitions or sequential development within the melody, sometimes a contrast of texture or of loudness or of rhythmic motif. Each particular technique in its particular context generates forward motion with a particular degree of strength, and the consequent arrival comes with a particular degree of prominence. The sense of arrival at bar 5 of Figure 3 is more vivid, for example, than that felt at bar 15. At places where the forward motion is relatively weak, the pairing is relatively loose; such loose relationships are a kind of instability that help generate stronger pairings at another architectonic level of the musical process. Each sonata-allegro movement has its own particular pattern of stronger and looser pairings. The strongest ones mark its most conspicuous points of arrival — its central events — and it is not possible to predict in advance where they will fall, even though they sound genuinely summoned when they happen.

Pieces in sonata-allegro form also differ from one another in the strength of the various articulations. Sometimes the onset of the bridge, for example, is so completely unarticulated that some analysts find it meaningless to speak of a bridge in these cases at all. Sometimes the end of the bridge and the beginning of the second theme is obscured. Although the beginnings of the development and recapitulation are usually clearly marked, the strength of these articulations also varies widely. This diversity is conspicuous to the attentive listener, and it implies that descriptions of the process in terms of a succession of parts (first theme, bridge, second theme, closing, development and recapitulation) or in terms of a melodic or harmonic structure are misleading.[21] While these labels often usefully refer to identifiable entities, they obscure both what distinguishes each sonata-allegro movement (namely, its distinctive pattern of stronger and weaker articulations and tighter and looser pairings) and also what each shares with the others (namely, the paired phrases and sections generated by the interaction of balance with forward thrust).

Both because the responding group is in some sense fresh and separate from the group to which it is responding and because the two groups as a pair introduce a fresh dynamic into the temporal process, sonata-allegro forms project a temporality in which change is real. Whether the change is great or small, however, it does not weaken the sense of continuity created by the way the first member of a group ends unstably and thrusts forward to its pair. The interaction of forward thrust with balancing sections creates the image of so moving from the present into the future that change and continuity do not contradict each other. In a Newtonian world and in the common-sense language controlled by its presuppositions (and in the images of Newtonian temporality presented in Bach's music), it is impossible for an occurrence to be both fully responsive to its past and yet have the quality of freshness that a decision implies. It is a tribute to the power of sonata-allegro form that it could make plausible a temporal process that the common-sense language contemporary with it would have had to reject, had it tried to think about it.

The paired phrases and sections of Classic-period music provide the best clue to the difference between the way present, past, and future events relate themselves to one another in the music of the late eighteenth century and the way they do in music of the Baroque period. Except in some of the dance movements, Baroque phrases are successive. They follow one another like links on a chain, without forming pairs. The third phrase is related to the second no differently from the way the second is related to the first. Because the motivic play is pervasive, because the imitative voices overlap one another and because the onset of a new phrase is often dovetailed into the cadence ending the previous one, Baroque music moves in a meter that has frequently, and aptly, been described as prose-like, while Classic meter, by contrast, is poetic. The same contrast characterizes the overall structure: Classic sections balance one another and form pairs, and Baroque ones do not. Like the phrases within a section, the sections of a *da capo* aria follow one another like the links on a chain, while the exposition and development in the sonata-allegro form are separated just as strongly as are the *da capo* aria's sections, yet form some sort of higher-level grouping. Both the articulations at the end of the aria's sections and those at the end of the Classical exposition seriously undermine a sense of inevitability: what follows the articulation bespeaks genuine change, and does not seem to be determined by what has preceded it. The difference between the Baroque and Classical sense of change at these points, however, is considerable: in the one, the forward thrust felt at the end of a section is so much less than it is within the section that change seems to be bought at the price of discontinuity. In the other, the forward thrust sparking the gap is as strong at the end of the section as it is at the end of a first phrase of a pair within the section, and so when the next section begins, the fresh event bespeaking genuine change is responsive to and palpably continuous with its past. In short, Baroque music in general offers an image of a temporal process in which the present seems most relevant to the future where it most controls the future and the principle of determination is clearly known; Classical music offers an image in which the present is as relevant to the future as it ever is in Baroque music and far more relevant on higher architectronic levels, but the future is summoned (and not determined) by its past.

3. Temporality in Romantic Music

Romantic music in general seems to evoke Classical temporality in order to reject or transcend it. Romantic composers continue, intensify and in the end transform the Classical composers' concern with that which is unique. Their music, like Classic sonata-allegro movements and unlike Baroque music, does not exemplify a process in which all events are analogous to mechanically caused events and in which individuality is subordinated to principles that make order universal. It is as though they believed that the late seventeenth and early eighteenth centuries' preoccupation with order so subordinated individuals to something extrinsic to themselves that what made each of them itself, himself or herself was suppressed. Unlike Classic sonata movements, however, Romantic music does not exemplify a process that resembles a free self creating an empirically visible future which adequately fulfills both the past and the self. It is as though the Romantics were disillusioned with the confidence and hope that preceded the French Revolution, and sensed that the late eighteenth century's preoccupation with publicly manifest events suppressed the irreducibly private depths of human experience.

Thinkers like Friedrich Schelling believed that the temporal process exemplified by Romantic music uncovered and celebrated what was spiritual in both human experience and nature. The spiritual depths, he was persuaded by Kant, could be known neither through empirical experience nor through concepts. But music (and the arts in general) could express what eluded discursive language, enabling listeners to feel what could not be conceptualized. According to Schelling's *System of Transcendental Idealism* (1800), what was to be expressed and felt was the most fundamental activity of the ego or deepest self. While Kant, forced by the logic of his analysis of reason, postulated such a self but did not believe it could in any way be described or known, Schelling tried to intimate what it was like by saying that its fundamental activity was an intuition that lay beyond the distinction between an unconscious, mechanically caused action and a conscious, freely chosen action. Such an activity could be understood as a product of neither a necessity nor a decision. It was basic to the ego because it enabled the self to transcend the following apparent contradiction: if human beings were part of nature, then they decided what they were caused to decide, and human freedom was an illusion; if the human mind imposed its categories on nature (as per Kant), then empirical objects of knowledge only appeared to be caused, and necessity in nature and human knowledge of natural objects were both illusory. Only if there was some activity or intuition in which there was no difference between necessity and freedom were both knowledge and free decisions, both causality in nature and human responsibility for one's actions, possible. According to Schelling's *System of Transcendental Idealism*, the artistic intuition was the one in which such an identity occurred, and the listener who heard this identity was in the presence of the self's most fundamental way of being. Totally unlike anything in Newton's universe, such a deepest self could not at all be understood by analogy to natural objects or laws, but music, art and poetry could be a window to it.[22]

Concepts drawn from Schelling's philosophical model provide an apt metaphor for some of the music written in the early nineteenth century. The theme for the set of variations in the third movement of Beethoven's "Archduke" Trio (Op. 97, 1811), for example, can be said to project an atemporality that is analogous to the deepest self's way of being. Movements like this one exerted a powerful influence on other nineteenth-century composers, who tried to achieve something of its effect in their own ways.

Superficially, the phrase structure of the theme for the Op. 97 slow movement resembles the shape of a typical Mozartian theme. It con-

FIGURE 5

L. van Beethoven, Trio in B-flat for Violin, Cello and Piano, Op. 97, third movement

sists of an eight-bar phrase played by the piano, the repetition of this phrase played by the violin, cello and piano, a new eight-bar phrase (piano) and the repetition of the last four bars of this phrase (violin, cello and piano). Each eight-bar phrase consists of a pair of four-bar subphrases, and each four-bar subphrase is internally divided into two-bar units. The first phrase (bars 1–8) ends unstably, like a Mozartian first phrase. But here the resemblance stops. Bar 9 sounds like the beginning of a phrase paired to the first one, but because the two phrases end exactly alike, they do not form an antecedent–consequent pair. The second phrase replicates the first's unstable ending and thereby raises the level of tension. The third phrase (bars 17–24), instead of absorbing that instability, and forming a pair with the preceding material, continues to intensify the instability as though the preceding phrase had not ended at all. In a typical Classical sonata-allegro theme, we would hear two waves, the second being pushed along by the first and the second reaching both its own goal and the goal of the previous phrase. The theme for the "Archduke" variations gives us the outward appearance of two waves (bars 1–16 and 17–28), each divided into two smaller waves, but in fact we hear a single wave that continues to get bigger and bigger until bar 21, and then subsides. The peak in bars 20–21 (repeated in bars 24–25) uses a rising motif that is used to heighten intensity throughout the theme (bars 2–3, 4–5, 10–11, 12–13, 18–19). The motif is at its most intense in bars 20–21, but an event that would absorb this intensity does not materialize. The music calms down, but an event generated by the mounting tension of bars 1–21, and at the same time demarcated by an articulating cadence, does not take place. The theme's peak is not the arrival of a goal, but the moment of greatest intensity. In the midst of the subsequent calming gesture, we hear a *crescendo* (bar 22) that seems to be carrying us once more toward a goal. But on the very note where the goal would be reached, we hear not the culminating *forte* that would bespeak arrival, but a sudden *piano* (bar 23). Nowhere do we get an event that can be heard as the future determined by the past (as in Bach's music) or summoned by the past (as in Classical paired sections).

Because the music cannot be heard as moving along a line toward a goal and then arriving at the goal, it cannot present the image of a publicly manifest event happening in response to its past and actualizing the deciding self. It is as though the motion implied by the process of intensification were inward instead of forward; although the theme begins as if it were an image of moving horizontally to a publicly manifest event, it imperceptibly changes into an image of penetrating deeper and deeper into a single point.

The image does not suggest that we are moving closer and closer to a point (that way of describing the process implies a kind of linear motion which the phrases refuse to suggest), but rather that we feel more and more the presence and force of this point. That of whose presence we are aware with increasing intensity neither changes nor causes change. When we are at the peak, we have gotten nowhere in the outer-world temporal process beyond when we were at the beginning: the motif in bars 20–21 is identical to the one used in bar 2, and it is set on the same pitches an octave higher. The gesture that begins the musical process reappears as and is identified with the gesture articulating its peak. Consequently, the contrast between preparing an event and actualizing it — the contrast essential to Classical paired phrases — is suppressed. Instead, the contrast between prior and subsequent gestures is the contrast of feeling the force of an atemporal reality — Schelling would call it the point of identity of necessity and freedom intuited by the deepest self — with less and then greater intensity.

The process of intensification presupposes an awareness of prior gestures as prior and of subsequent ones as subsequent, and in that sense the process is a temporal one. But the nature of this temporal process is very different from that projected by Baroque and Classical music, for the feeling of deepest penetration into the self's basic intuition of itself is neither an eventful nor a determined occurrence. It is not summoned by the past nor shaped by a deciding self; still less is it determined by the way things are. Using Schelling's terms, one can say that the self's basic intuition is a point beyond the distinction between that which is determined and that which is free, and so feeling it and its force is beyond the distinction between the process of a past determining the future by the operation of immutable laws (a process which Bach's music metaphorically exemplifies) and the process of a self making a decision and shaping a future that is responsive both to itself and to the past (a process which Classical sonata-allegro movements metaphorically exemplify).

The tempo for the "Archduke" variations is slow, and slow movements are generally thought to be more meditative than fast ones. Yet Haydn's and Mozart's slow movements maintain the same distinction between summoning and realizing gestures that characterize their sonata-allegro movements and that is absent from the slow movement in the "Archduke" Trio. Beethoven's fast movements also depend on this distinction, but in some of the later ones, realizing gestures are anticipated but never articulated. These pieces suggest a

FIGURE 6

Beethoven, Sonata in C Minor for Piano, Op. 111, first movement

FIGURE 7

Beethoven, Sonata, Op. 111/i

violent struggle in which the self seeks to actualize itself by shaping outer-world events, but fails.[23] This failure shifts our attention away from the eventful occurrence presented by Classical paired sections and forces us to focus on the self that is presupposed but unillumined by Classical movements.

The first movement of Beethoven's Piano Sonata in C Minor, Op. 111 (1822), is a good example. In it one hears a continuous search for events that will genuinely satisfy the past that summons them. Continuously it gropes for the climax that would symbolize the power of a free self to make a decision which would at once make the self concrete and give the strivings of the past a satisfactory completion. Again and again, we hear failure; sometimes the climactic moment is filled with the harsh, strident sound of a diminished-seventh chord (e.g. bar 132 and bar 146; see Figure 6); sometimes the mounting tension simply dissipates without ever arriving at anything that precipitates out of the flux as an identifiable event (e.g. bars 47–51; see Figure 7); sometimes closure is almost achieved, but a new surge of energy erupts too abruptly to allow us to feel that the completion was in any way satisfactory (e.g. bars 27–29, 35, and 99–100). The ending of the movement (bars 150–58) provides a strange, relaxed benediction, strange because it does not seem to have been earned. This blessing over the struggle of the inner self to realize itself and impose its own shape on the outer world transforms the struggle's failure into a victory. It suggests that any apparent success in creating manifest events that genuinely respond to the past and correspond to the self would be only apparent: no manifest event can ever be big enough, right enough to do justice to the energy of past and self that works it up. Any event that to a previous age might have stood for success would in fact be a failure, because it would be a delusion. Struggle itself is the only victory. And it is a true triumph, for it displays the self accepting its need and its inability to express itself outwardly without retreating from the one nor letting itself be overwhelmed by the other. The struggle and failure to make onself actual is the form that actualization must take. Beethoven's benediction suggests that to continue the struggle in the face of what the late eighteenth century would have regarded as a failure is in fact a success, though obviously not a publicly manifest one.

According to Kant's philosophy, the atemporal transcendental self actualizes itself in a temporal empirical self and its achievements (and Classical paired phrases project an image of this process). In Beethoven's Op. 111/i, working toward but never achieving an arrival focuses attention on the interface between that which is relentlessly temporal (the struggle to actualize oneself fully by bringing public events to a satisfactory completion) and that which just as stubbornly cannot be (the self in its failure to become fully actual). In spite of its failure, the self, in this image of the temporal process, does not retreat from temporality and seek fulfillment in some atemporal reality because struggling to actualize itself and satisfactorily shape public events is evidently the only way the self can be real. Moreover, sustaining the struggle in spite of inevitable defeat (in public eyes) is itself a kind of fulfillment, though a kind fundamentally different from what the late eighteenth century envisioned.

The later Beethoven is usually regarded as a transitional figure between the Classic and Romantic styles. Although he did not abandon the high Classic style, he extended it in ways that later nineteenth-century composers took up and made the hallmark of their style, rejecting Classic temporality as they did so. Two aspects of the Romantics' style that indicate the kind of temporality projected by their music are the nature of climaxes and the preference for gradual transformations over clear articulations. One cannot, of course, make valid generalizations about the temporal process in all the varied pieces of Romantic music only on the basis of these two features. But one can suggest what these features in general imply about temporality. In studying an individual piece, one is then in a position to determine how the interaction of these techniques with other aspects of the piece modify these general implications. The following paragraphs will point out some of these general implications so that later chapters will be able to compare Beethoven's climaxes and transformations with their Romantic descendants.

Climaxes in Romantic music differ from their Classic predecessors in two fundamental ways. First, they usually occur within the same musical gesture that generates them. Second, they generally define themselves as moments when the rate of increase of energy becomes a negative rate without first attaining a resolution or absorbing the forward thrust of the prior material. In other words, the climax is the moment when the sense of building pressure is most intense; energy may still be developed after the climax, but the rate at which it grows is noticeably slower than it is before the climax, and no fulfillment or arrival takes place before this slowdown occurs. For instance, in the first movement of Felix Mendolssohn's D Minor Trio, Op. 49 (Figure 8), the rate of intensification begins to slow down in bar 91, where the harmony becomes less agitated; although the forward pressure continues to build, it is building less quickly, and by bar 107 it has begun to wane. The slowdown bespeaks a kind of relaxation, but no resolu-

FIGURE 8
F. Mendelssohn, Trio in D Minor for Violin, Cello and Piano, Op. 49, first movement

tion; no energy-absorbing event takes place.

The first characteristic of the typical Romantic climax makes it impossible for it to express an event; the second makes it impossible for it to express fulfillment. In the sort of temporal process that is projected by the Classic paired sections, an eventful occurrence stands out of the temporal flux, at once related to its antecedents and cut off from them by a decision that interjects something unpredictable and fresh into the temporal flow. The event is both continuous with its past and a moment when change begins. It is both rationally intelligible and fundamentally unique. The Romantic climax offers no such moment. Rather, it represents the most profound intensification of the forces that are already in play. That which these forces seem to be preparing never actually takes place. Energies dissipate without generating a public event that would actualize a decision-making self and the goal of its past.

The change in the nature of the climax changes fundamentally that for which it is a metaphor. The arrivals that characterize Classical paired sections figuratively exemplify the process of the self making decisions, actualizing itself and shaping external reality so that the latter genuinely expresses the self. Because the Romantic climax reaches its peak without such an arrival, attention shifts from the process of actualization to the inner self struggling to make itself concrete in a recalcitrant outer world. This shift is perhaps the basis for the often made but somewhat vague comment that Romantic music is "subjective." This term would be misleading, however, if it were construed to mean that Romantic music offers a metaphor of the deepest self as such in isolation from all external reality. Rather, the process of building a Romantic climax is like the self exerting itself vis-à-vis some particular set of circumstances and continuing the struggle in the face of its failure. Building the climax suggests both the self's power and its utter difference from causal powers in the natural world. The climax itself is the end of the struggle not in that it is an image of arriving at the struggle's goal but in the sense of suggesting most explicitly the self's inability to shape that with which it is dealing and projecting most vividly the quality and power of the self's presence vis-à-vis that particular external reality.

As a metaphor for both the self's exertion and its ultimate lack of success, the Romantic climax connotes far more about the force of the self than does the success portrayed by Classical arrivals; to the nineteenth-century mind, the eighteenth-century's arrivals and successes must have seemed facile and naive. But the Romantic climax connotes very little about the external reality with which the self is dealing beyond its recalcitrance. Although a text or a program may specify the external pole of the struggle, it seems to be presupposed yet left generally undefined by the music itself in much the same way that an inner self is presupposed but not illumined in Classical music. And the Romantic climax connotes nothing about the deepest self as such beyond its energy, and even this aspect is always presented in terms of a specific direction.

The other technique that characterizes Romantic music is the gradual transformation and tendency to avoid clear-cut articulations.[24] Typically a climax is reached, the level of intensity tapers off, and the section whose focus is provided by the climax fades away. The motif used as the section winds down is gradually transformed into a new motif or into the accompaniment to a new theme, which builds a new climax, and this climax defines a new section. The passage in bars 109–19 of Figure 8 is an example of this procedure. Sometimes a strong cadence occurs, but what follows it behaves as if there had been none, and the material after the cadence is a continuation of, not a response to, what preceded it. In other words, such a cadence makes an articulation within a section, not between sections.

Sometimes one cannot avoid the suspicion that if the articulation between sections were clean and sharp, the music would simply halt. For the energy developing the Romantic climax has dissipated before the end of the section; there is so little residual tension at the low ebb between climaxes that if a firm cadence were stated at that point and the surface motion ceased, nothing would keep the music going. When it started up again, the new music would seem arbitrary and unmotivated, as if a new piece were beginning. The gradual transformation becomes crucial to the relationship between the present and the future because it is the chief means of continuity. Change is presented not as the necessary unfolding of the past's implications nor as a decisive response to the past, but as the outgrowth of the past. The music is like a living thing undergoing metamorphoses that are controlled neither by causal mechanisms nor by free decisions.

What is metamorphosing is the self, the particular quality of whose force changes as the nature of the particular outer-world reality against which it is exerting itself changes. The process of moving toward a Romantic climax exemplifies the process of the self's force, exerted in some particular (though musically unspecified) situation, becoming especially vivid and intense. The climax itself is an image of this particularized force at its peak. And moving away from the climax in a Romantic transformation is like the self backing off from participating in the first particular external situation and beginning to exert itself through a relationship with something else. This receding is not experienced as a decision, but simply as something that happens. It is not as though the self has the power from itself to transform one way of exerting and being itself into another. Nor is the transformation controlled by anything external to the self. We hear what the self undergoes, not what it decides to do and not what it is determined to be.

Although these metamorphoses obey no law external to themselves, and there are no criteria of orderly transformation shared by all Romantic pieces, they do not sound arbitrary or capricious. A Schelling would say that while change in Baroque temporality is controlled by the unconscious operation of unvarying laws and while change in Classic temporality is controlled by the conscious decision of a moral agent, change in Romantic temporality is controlled by that which is neither unconscious nor conscious.

For Schelling, the point of non-differentiation between consciousness and unconsciousness, or between freedom and necessity, is as radically atemporal as Newton's laws of motion or Kant's unactualized self. Nevertheless, just as the unconscious, natural law operates and becomes visible in a temporal process and as the free, moral agent concretizes itself temporally, so also this deepest point within the self manifests itself temporally — to the extent that it does become manifest. The process in which the force of the self, making itself felt through a particular relationship, becomes maximally intense (for which the Romantic climax is a metaphor) and then undergoes a gradual change as the objective pole of its awareness changes (for which the Romantic transformation is a metaphor) involves, after all, some sort of contrast between what is and what will be. Yet, totally unlike the other two atemporalities, Schelling's deepest self is always alienated from its temporal manifestation: no temporal event or series of events or patterns of events fully reveals or actualizes it. It owns its future in the sense that what it undergoes is not imposed on it from without, yet it cannot fully impose itself on its future, and so the future does not and cannot assume its shape. Thus, what comes to pass reveals the presence and force of the deepest self, and at the same time the incongruence between the concrete actuality that transpires and the self struggling to shape it implies that what happens also veils the deepest self. The process of change from what is to what comes to be serves the double function of revealing and hiding the self. For Schelling, the idea that this process reveals the self confirms its reality while the idea that it hides the self confirms its radical uniqueness, spirituality and utter difference from all forms of material reality. That the self perpetually moves toward and simultaneously recedes from view is its glory. The artistic intuition creates a product that presents the process of struggle, failure and renewed struggle; the work of art offers an image of the double process of revealing and hiding, and by doing so it (and only it, and not actual events in the concrete world) offers the possibility of a complete intuition of the self.[25]

While the later Beethoven and the early Romantics seem to believe that the self's failure to conjure up a future adequate to itself is in fact a victory, the later Romantics are less optimistic. The value put on the double process of revealing and hiding changes from positive to negative, and the mood of the music changes from one of courageous affirmation — courageous because of the inevitable failure of the struggle — to one of angry despair or grim resignation.

Johannes Brahms' "Edward" Ballade, Op. 20, No. 1 (1856), and his E-flat Rhapsody, Op. 119, No. 4 (1893), are good examples of late Romantic despair (though not all his music is so pessimistic). The Ballade retells musically a Scottish poem in which a son explains to his mother why his sword is so red. His story has two startling revelations: first, it turns out that he has killed his father, and, second, that he has done so at his mother's bidding. Brahms' version has three sections. In the first, the son and the mother address each other twice. In the second, a violent turmoil gathers. In it, a fragment of the mother's theme emerges from the depths and becomes the impulse that works up a furious lather. Within a single musical gesture, three peaks of intensity (bars 37–42) are attained, each of which should count as a climax. Each of the first two are surpassed, working the energy to a level that the third climax cannot contain. Consequently, the third peak sounds hollow. It cannot bear the weight of what called it into being. The climax sounds overdone, hence empty.

In nineteenth-century literature, the parricide is a son who rejects the place in society into which he is born and the structures that promise to make something of him. Feeling that the forms that would mold him are alien to his own true nature, he destroys them. He *must* murder the father and destroy the restrictions on his growth to have room, as the orphan does, to invent himself. The parricide cuts himself off from his past in order to allow his spirit free rein in shaping a future. But in Brahms' version, the concrete event that happens is not what was struggling to take shape. It is the sound of disillusionment. The third climax restates the mother's theme, suggesting that her will has triumphed. The emptiness of this climax suggests that the son is as alienated from the victory he has achieved (or suffered) as from the structures he has destroyed.

As the climax dies away, the music gradually transforms itself into a faltering restatement of the son's theme (the third section). Instead of blessing the struggle and failure, as does the coda in Beethoven's Sonata, Op. 111/i, it breathes gloom, bitterness and isolation from the entire world in which the protagonist deals with others.

Brahms' Rhapsody, Op. 119, No. 4, is one of the few pieces that begin using a major scale and end with a minor one. The mood of the opening is positive. Yet it unleashes more energy than it can harness. Each of the piece's sections attempts to articulate a climax that is big enough to do justice to these energies, but before that toward which the energies grope is actualized, the energies begin to dissipate. Again and again, we hear a climax that is not an arrival but is rather the moment just before the energies begin to wane. The opening theme reaches a peak of intensity in the diminished-seventh chord in bar 19 (Figure 9), but before a satisfactory resolution can take place, the music cascades downward into a calmer section (bars 21–40). This section does not contain the arrival of that toward which bars 1–20 are working, but is instead an interlude between the opening theme and its reprise (bars 41–64). The interlude ends with a surge whose goal is the return of the opening theme. The return is experienced as an arrival, but the sense of fulfillment is vitiated when, in bar 56, the tension reaches a new peak and the energy bursts through the confines of the fulfilling event. The unresolved tension is too great to permit the section to sound closed when it is over, and the deceptive cadence (bars 60–61), rising figure (even changing register in bar 63) and six-four chord accompanying the final note (bars 63–64) are consonant with the section's inconclusiveness. The next section (bars 65–92) increases the level of frustration, because it too reaches a peak (bars 81–83) and then ends with its tensions suspended in mid-air, as if they did not know where to direct themselves.

FIGURE 9

Brahms, Rhapsody in E-flat, Op. 119, No. 4

At the next appearance of the opening theme (bars 153–67) the motifs are fragmented and scattered all over the keyboard; once again a fulfilling event is both suggested and denied. During the interlude (bars 168–216) between this statement and the final statement of the opening theme (bars 217–30; see Figure 10), the piece reaches its highest peak (bars 206–16). The return of the opening theme is a fulfillment, but it is not big enough. It is so paled by and is so inadequate to the forces generating it that the lapse into the minor mode in bars 231–32 seems altogether fitting. The hope for resolution has

FIGURE 10
Brahms, Rhapsody in E-flat, Op. 119, No. 4

proved vain. The mood becomes dark. The ending is a ferocious wail that envelopes the whole piece in grim futility.

The Beethoven Sonata, Op. 111/i, and the Brahms Ballade and Rhapsody are musical processes in which expectations are set up that are not fulfilled. All three suggest a struggle to achieve a genuine resolution that would do justice to the past's strivings and to the self's attempts to actualize itself.And in all of them the struggle ends without such a resolution taking place. Yet Beethoven, in the coda, suggests a courageous affirmation in the face of non-resolution. Just as for Schelling the incongruence between the concrete events that actually happen and the self struggling to shape them confirms the spirituality of the self, so Beethoven's benedictory coda suggests that the strivings are to be affirmed precisely because they do not succeed in establishing a resolution: the non-resolution confirms that what is working toward a resolution is not merely forceful but is in fact too forceful to be contained within or adequately expressed by any finite, resolving event. In the Brahms pieces, by contrast, the endings sink into unredeemed despair — unredeemed because the struggles are fruitless in every sense and from every perspective. The difference between the Beethoven and the Brahms examples is paralleled by the difference between Schelling and Arthur Schopenhauer. In paragraph 52 of *The World as Will and Idea* (1818), Schopenhauer says that music manifests and expresses the ceaseless, blind striving that underlies all reality. The striving is blind because it can project no goal that would really satisfy it and finally objectify ultimate reality; it is ceaselessly because it is purposeless. The music he has in mind has great forward thrust, but never attains a satisfying resolution. The contrast between past and future is a contrast between the struggles of the one and the failure of the other to contain events that would consummate and thereby warrant such an exertion. Nothing is ever enough. The non-resolution activates the silence into which it falls. And the silence is experienced as despair because what needs to happen to make the past worthwhile does not and apparently cannot happen.

For some people, the feeling of longing is the most human of feelings. Samuel Butler poked fun at this attitude in his paraphrase, "Better to have loved and lost than not to have lost at all." These people embrace Romantic music because it celebrates longing. Schopenhauer, however, seemed to regret that unending longing is the ultimate reality. For him, Romantic music is important not because it celebrates and sustains unsatisfied yearning, but because it objectifies the process of experiencing the contrast between a struggling present and a non-consummating future as despair. To objectify the process is to make it into an object that is detached from oneself, and in this way Romantic music offers the opportunity to transcend ceaseless yearning. Schopenhauer's Romantic music is like Baroque music in one critical respect: both are a means of release from those experiences to which the contrast between present and future is relevant; both are a path to an atemporal perspective. But the differences are also critical: from the timeless perspective of the Baroque, the temporal process becomes orderly and hence meritorious. But in Schopenhauer's system and in the temporal process for which Brahms' Ballade and Rhapsody are metaphors, the process of moving from struggle to failure has no positive value; it is to be rejected; one seeks release from it; and, once released, one will neither want nor need to remember it in any way.

Notes

1. I. Kant, *Critique of Pure Reason* (1781; trans. Norman Kemp Smith, 1929); G.W.F. Hegel, *Phenomenology of Mind* (1807; trans. J.B. Baillie, second edition, 1931; see also Alexandre Kojeve, *Introduction to the Reading of Hegel* [1969], ch. 5); E. Husserl, *Cartesian Meditations* (1950; trans. Dorion Cairns, 1970); M. Heidegger, *Being and Time* (1927; trans. John Macquarrie and Edward Robinson, 1962); H. Bergson, *Matter and Memory* (fifth edition, 1908; trans. N.M. Paul and W.S. Palmer, 1912) and *Time and Free Will* (1889; trans. R.L. Pogson, 1913); Georges Poulet, *Studies in Huamn Time* (1950; trans. Elliott Coleman, 1956); H. Marshall McLuhan, *Through the Vanishing Point* (1968). See also Jacqueline De Romilly, *Time in Greek Tragedy* (1968); Ricardo Quinones, *The Renaissance Discovery of Time* (1972); and Jerome Buckley, *The Triumph of Time: A Study of the Victorian Concepts of Time, History, Progress and Decadence* (1966).

2. Suzanne Langer in *Feeling and Form* (1953) talks of musical duration as an image of "lived" time. She says that "music spreads out time for our direct and complete apprehension, by letting our hearing monopolize it [time] — organize, fill and shape it, all alone. . . . *Music makes time audible, and its form and continuity sensible*" (pp. 109–10; italics hers). She evidently assumes that time is a given that is the same for everyone, and this assumption implies that music is better or less good according to how effectively it makes this fixed structure of reality audible. If one recognizes that a variety of understandings of the temporal process inform different people's experiences, then one is led to ask, as she does not ask, what the particular time is that a particular piece makes audible.

3. For elaborations of the idea that meaning in music is the relations of the sounds to one another, see, among other books, Victor Zuckerkandl, *The Sense of Music* (1959), pp. 11–21; Leonard Meyer, *Emotion and Meaning in Music* (1956), pp. 32–38; and Edward Lippman, *A Humanistic Philosophy of Music* (1977), pp. 80–160. Lippman explicitly connects musical relationships to the inner experience of duration and temporality. Through a careful and sensitive phenomenological analysis of the experience of sound, he argues persuasively that "Music is in short a medium that is remarkably adequate to arouse and represent and articulate the feeling of inner duration" (p. 133) and "Sound makes us particularly aware of our consciousness, of its life and flow" (p. 138). The present book's analyses of particular styles, forms and individual pieces both presuppose and confirm Lippman's position.

4. Leonard Meyer's *Emotion and Meaning in Music* is based on the premise that affect is generated in musical experience by arousing and fulfilling expectations. When an expectation is temporarily inhibited, he says, affect becomes more intense. Fulfillment that follows a delay is more deeply satisfying than immediate gratification. His theory applies nicely to many eighteenth- and nineteenth-century pieces that have a view of the temporal process similar to his own, in which concrete fulfillment means a completion that is both desirable and concretely realizable and the undesirableness of non-fulfillment implies that the contrast between what is and what will be is also a contrast between what is and what ought to be. It illumines less well the experience of hearing music in which the move from expectation to fulfillment is localized and not spread over large stretches of music. It is no accident, for example, that he does not talk about Palestrina. A suspension in a Palestrina motet generates the expectation of its resolution, and a listener familiar with his style knows that the resolution will be stepwise, downward and immediate: the move from expectation to fulfillment is localized, not spread over a whole passage. In hearing an entire passage or the relation of one passage to the next in Palestrina, one is aware of a contrast between what is and what is coming, but one does not hear the contrast as a discrepancy between incompleteness and completion or between what is and what ought to be: Although one is aware of a difference between the present and the future, the move from the one to the other is not a move from undesirable non-fulfillment to satisfying fulfillment. Thus, the temporal process projected by Palestrina's music is quite different from the temporal process presented by music in which large sections are organized into a pattern of expectation and fulfillment. When music, such as Palestrina's, exemplifies a temporal process that is different from the one Meyer presupposes, his theory is silent about the way it can matter to us.

5. The concept of metaphorical samples is developed by Nelson Goodman in his *Languages of Art* (1968), ch. 2, pp. 49–95. Goodman's theory is summarized and clarified and applied to music in a lecture by Professor Monroe Beardsley of Temple University, "Understanding Music," delivered at Johns Hopkins University in 1979. Beardsley proposes that music works exemplify various "modes of continuation" and that this kind of exemplification is their most important one. Beardsley's lecture is published in *On Criticizing Music: Five Philosophical Perspectives*, ed. Kingsley Price (1981).

6. Donald N. Ferguson in *Music as Metaphor: The Elements of Expression* (1960) contends that music, like poetry, offers us metaphors for "the very stuff . . . of experience as it lives . . . in our minds." In spite of his efforts to ground this contention in the analyses of particular pieces Ferguson is, unfortunately, never very precise about that for which music is a metaphor. One suspects his work would have benefited from Goodman's penetrating analysis of metaphorical exemplification. See Leonard Meyer's review of Ferguson's book in the *Journal of the American Musicology Society*, vol. 15 (1962), p. 236.

7. Particularly helpful in this respect is *On Metaphor*, ed. by Sheldon Sacks (1979) and Marcus Hester, "Metaphor and Aspect Seeing," *Journal of Aesthetics and Art Criticism*, vol. 25 (1966), pp. 205–12.

8. Hester, *op. cit.*, p. 207, deals with Shakespeare's metaphor of time as a beggar (*Troilus and Cressida*, III, iii, 145–50). Hester uses the term "aspect-blindness" for the absence of insight into those aspects of time and beggars that are related by the metaphor.

9. Edward Lowinsky, "Taste, Style and Ideology in Eighteenth-Century Music" in Earl R. Wasserman, ed., *Aspects of the Eighteenth Century* (1965), pp. 179–81, suggests that Bach's music is a perfect symbol of Leibniz's universe: a Bach motif, like a Leibnizian monad, is characterized by energy and self-consistency; the action of a motif, like a monad, follows its own inner principle, yet it mirrors the whole, for the whole is generated by the operation of the monad working in accord with its nature. "The logic of Bach's continuity can be defined in the same terms in which Leibniz defines the monad: 'Every present state of a simple substance [monad] is naturally a consequence of its preceding state, in such a way that its present is big with its future' " (p. 181). Lowinsky sees Bach's polyphony as analogous to the harmonious operation of the many monads: "As the multiplicity of monads is regulated by a pre-established harmony so is the multiplicity of Bach's temporal and polyphonic figurations governed by the pre-existent laws of counterpoint and harmony" (p. 180). This analogy is flawed: Leibniz's doctrine of the pre-established harmony is that each monad is created in such a way that operating in accord with its own intrinsic nature is harmonious with all other activities. By appealing to pre-existent laws of counterpoint and harmony to explain Bach's polyphony, Lowinsky implies that a law extrinsic to a given motif governs its behaviour, and such an extrinsic principle is foreign to Leibniz's philosophy. Lowinsky might better have said that when two or more motifs are simultaneously present, each exerts the force of its own nature, yet the intrinsic nature of each is such that their joint operation is harmonious. The harmony is foreordained not because the operation of the motifs is controlled by the pre-existent laws of counterpoint but because the behavior of each motif is governed by its own nature and is thereby determined in a way that, it turns out, is harmonious with the behavior of other intrinsically governed motifs. The principles of counterpoint may be said to describe (but not govern) the resulting harmoniousness. Lowinsky does not go on to say, as one might, that God, being God, could not have created monads whose intrinsically determined behavior as a whole would not have been harmonious, while Bach, being human, presumably could have created motifs whose intrinsically controlled behaviours might have been discordant. Bach's music is called divine, perhaps, because he lapsed so seldom into discord or forced his motifs to behave in a way contrary to their intrinsic nature. One might also go on to say, as Lowinsky does not, that, for Leibniz, to recognize that the collective operation of the monads is in fact harmonious is to understand the mind of God, for such a recognition presupposes an awareness of what God thinks the nature of harmony to be. To hear Bach's polyphony as harmonious is to hear what his age believed to be objectively harmonious, that is, harmonious by the same standard of harmony that the collective operation of monads is harmonious. For this reason, Bach's polyphony can be said to mirror the mind of God. Its beauty from the intrinsic beauty of God's thinking.

Lowinsky argues convincingly that the idea of an analogy between music and philosophy is of a piece with Baroque thinking (p. 181) and that some of Bach's friends were familiar with Leibnizian thought (pp. 183–84). The latter argument is probably unnecessary, for while Lowinsky's analogy of Bach's motifs to Leibniz's monads has the advantage of linking the music to a specific philosophy, Bach's style is of a piece with rationalist premises in general, and not simply to Leibniz's particular delineation of them.

10. *Music, the Arts and Ideas* (1967), pp. 24–27.

11. Georges Poulet, *op. cit.*, describes the efforts of Diderot, Rousseau and other eighteenth-century philosophers to think themselves into eternal, non-temporal moments that transcend memory of the past and hope for the future. The change entailed in transcending temporality is, of course, totally undetermined by an event in the temporal process. Hume's idea that change happens without causality — because when one says that an event causes another event, all one can mean by "causes" is that the second event follows the first, even if it is the case that many events similar to the first are followed by many events similar to the second — flatly contradicted eighteenth-century common sense and its language.

12. See Alexandre Kojeve, "A Note on Eternity, Time and Concept" in *op. cit.*, pp. 100–49, for an analysis of the concept of human temporality in Hegel's *Phänomenologie des Geistes* (1807) and a comparison of Hegel's analysis to Kant's assumptions.

13. Christopher Ballantine, "Beethoven, Hegel and Marx," *The Music Review*, vol. 33 (1972), pp. 34–46, studies the similarities between Haydn's, Mozart's and Beethoven's sonata-allegro forms and Hegel's concept of the dialectic that shapes the temporal process.

14. Charles Rosen, *The Classical Style* (1972), p. 44, identifies the Classical style, created by Haydn and Mozart, as one in which "a dramatic effect seemed at once surprising and logically motivated." The expression, "logically motivated," presumably does not mean that one set of musical events generates the next in the way that the premises of a syllogism generate a conclusion, but rather that the second event is motivated and prompted by the prior ones (and not by the text or anything extrinsic to the music) and that the second is justified by the first while the first is in some sense completed or carried forward or resolved by the second.

15. The term "paired phrases" refers to the same phenomenon for which Rosen uses the term "articulated periodic structure" (*op. cit.*, pp. 57–58). The terms "antecedent" and "consequent" are used by many analysts to refer to the first and second phrases, respectively, in a pair. Some analysts restrict the usage of "antecedent" and "consequent" to two juxtaposed phrases which have the same melody at their beginning and differ at their ends in that the first closes on the dominant, the second in the tonic. Other analysts use "antecedent" and "consequent" to refer to any set of two phrases that form a pair with each other, even if their melodies are not identical. The term "paired phrases" has two advantages over both "periodic structure" and "antecedent–consequent": "First, "paired phrases" calls attention to the dynamic relation holding the two phrases together. Second, higher-level sections are also paired to one another, and using the same term for the relations between phrases as for the relation between sections calls attention to the significant analogy between the two kinds or levels of relationships. This analogy is vital to the sonata-allegro process and emphasizing it is probably the most significant feature that differentiates the interpretation of sonata form presupposed in this study from that of Rosen.

16. The way a highly organized paired-phrases structure creates pressure toward a more fluent section is elaborated in connection with the appearance of this phenomenon in Beethoven's Quartet, Op. 59/1/i, in chapter I, part 2, section (1), subsection (i) below.

17. The relative stability of the second theme in comparison to the first is a function of a number of different features, not all of which are present in every movement. These features and the frequency with which they occur in the music of Beethoven's contemporaries are listed in chapter III, part 1, section (2), subsection (i), "The Two Themes."

18. Theodor Adorno writes as though the musical subject is a metaphor for a self that maintains an identity with itself through various transformations. See Rose Rosengard Suboptnik, "Adorno's Diagnosis of Beethoven's Late Style: Early

Symptoms of a Fatal Condition," *Journal of the American Musicological Society*, vol. 29 (1976), pp. 248–49.

19. It is perhaps because Classical paired phrases and paired sections can serve as a metaphor for the process of an agent making decisions and molding events that Mozart's operas impress one as dramatic, while Baroque operas, with their juxtaposed scenes that are only loosely related musically, seems more pictorial or, when the juxtaposed pictures contrast violently, theatrical. Joseph Kerman, in *Opera as Drama* (1956), pp. 73–79, 95–98, and Rosen, *op. cit.*, pp. 51, 289–325, call attention to the dramatic possibilities latent within sonata form. Rosen explains the affinity between the form and the stage by emphasizing that *opera buffa* is one of the important sources of the sonata style. David Linthicum, in "Verdi's *Falstaff* and Classical Sonata Form," *The Music Review*, vol. 39 (1978), pp. 39–53, interprets the opening scene of *Falstaff* as a sonata form. Given his awareness that the form has the power to project a convincing psychological interaction of characters, one finds it odd that he describes sonata form as an "aural manifestation of current philosophical tenets, wherein all relative existence was viewed in the light of linear, mechanistic principles of causation."

20. See I. Kant, *op. cit.*, pp. 167–68 and 381–82.

21. Rosen, *op. cit.*, pp. 30–98, especially 30, 58, 64, 69 and 70. William S. Newman, *The Sonata in the Classical Era* (1963), pp. 143–58, and Leonard Ratner, "Harmonic Aspects of Classical Form," *Journal of the American Musicological Society*, vol. 2 (1949), pp. 159–68, also find such labels misleading. In emphasizing the harmonic structure of sonata forms, Ratner obscures them less than do the nineteenth-century theorists who describe a sonata form almost exclusively in terms of melodic contrasts and repetitions. But a corresponding preoccupation with the harmonic structure may hide the important analogy between paired phrases and paired sections (Ratner is aware of this analogy with regard to Beethoven, see his "Eighteenth-Century Theories of Musical Period Structure," *Musical Quarterly*, vol. 42 [1956], pp. 439–54). It may also hide the way a unique set of tight and loose pairings and strong and weak articulations characterize each movement as the particular entity it is (again, Ratner is aware of the importance of comparatively weak articulations in Beethoven's music; see his "Key Definition — A Structural Issue in Beethoven's Music," *Journal of the American Musicological Society*, vol. 23 [1970], p. 483).

22. Selections from Schelling's *System of Transcendental Idealism* are translated in Albert Hofstadter and Richard Kuhns, eds., *Philosophies of Art and Beauty* (1974), pp. 347–77. See especially pp. 361–65. See also Friedrich Schleiermacher's remarks on music and feeling religious depths in his *Weihnachtsfeier* (1805; trans. T. Tice as *Christmas Eve* [1967], pp. 46–47; 85).

23. Theodor Adorno makes a similar point. He sees nineteenth-century music, beginning with Beethoven's third-period style, as losing the quality of organic wholeness that characterized music during the Classic period. (Adorno emphasizes the universality of the decisions and fulfillments exemplified by the Classic sonata-allegro process to an extent that the music itself may not justify.) According to him, modern reality, like nineteenth-century music, is fragmented; that is, what the self must do, acting out of inner necessity, no longer coincides with outer, objective reality, shaped as it is by forces intrinsic to the self. Consequently, what happens is ultimately arbitrary, however rationally the description of empirical reality may seem, because the effective forces have no genuine connection with the human, and at the same time the human self suffers a loss of true individuality because its putative expressions, however unique they may be, are not in fact guided by inner necessity. See his *Introduction to the Sociology of Music* (1962; trans. E.B. Ashton, 1976) and Rose Rosengard Subotnik, *op. cit.* and "The Historical Structure: Adorno's 'French' Model for the Criticism of Nineteenth-century Music," *Nineteenth-Century Music*, vol. 2 (1978–79), pp. 36–60.

24. Nineteenth-century composers like Wagner and Mahler and theorists of nineteenth-century music like Schoenberg and Carl Dalhaus explicitly recognize the importance of the transition in endowing Romantic music with its distinguishing character and in breaking down the symmetries of Classic paired groups. For a succinct summary of these matters, see Richard Swift's review, "Mahler's Ninth and Cooke's Tenth," *Nineteenth-Century Music*, vol. 2 (1978), pp. 165–67.

25. See Schelling, *op. cit.*, pp. 365, 371–73. Schelling's contemporary, Johann Gottlieb Fichte, in his *The Vocation of Man* (1800; trans. R.M. Chisholn, 1956), was also aware that actions do not fully reveal their agent and also believed that to recognize the gap between actions and their agent was to ascribe glory to man. "We act," he says, "not because we know [that the external world exists or what its nature is], but we know because we are called upon to act" (p. 98). Feeling summoned to free, responsible acts is a matter of faith; one cannot demonstrate the validity of this feeling, for it is more basic than any principles one might invoke to demonstrate its validity. Fichte implies that both one's actions and the world are less basic than the self and its primordial feeling of being summoned to moral activity. It is the latter that reveals and determines the truth about our actions and the world, and not the other way around. Therefore, one can see actions as manifesting the self only if one already knows the self.

Preliminary:
Beethoven, Revolution and Temporality

PEOPLE WHO are fascinated with revolutions and heroism often think about Beethoven and his music in those terms. The categories suggest themselves because many of the techniques he used seem to have been revolutionarily innovative and many of the gestures in his music seem heroic. Moreover, his brusque and sometimes coarse behavior toward his aristocratic patrons, as well as some of his comments comparing his worth to theirs, has suggested to biographers that in his political attitude he had affinities with some revolutionaries.[1] Circumstances and temperament combined to make him something of a rebel: they forced him to remain his own man, and he sold his composing, teaching and performing on his own terms without becoming a servant in either an aristocratic or ecclesiastical post. His *Fidelio* celebrated the (middle-class) forces that revolted against tyranny, and his Ninth Symphony celebrated universal brotherhood as the goal of such revolt.

But descriptions of Beethoven's music in terms of revolution and heroism need to incorporate some counter-data. His lesser known or properly forgotten Viennese contemporaries experimented with high Classic forms in ways that sometimes were at least as radical as Beethoven's departures from the style of Haydn and Mozart. Some of the innovations often attributed to Beethoven (such as using keys other than the dominant for the second theme in major-mode sonata-allegro movements, or not putting a crisp caesura between the bridge and second theme, or not repeating the exposition) were in fact tried by others before him.[2] Because Beethoven's innovations and his use of others' experiments make more sense to twentieth-century ears and minds, we are likely to assume it was his and not his contemporaries' influence that guided the development of music in the nineteenth century. But these facts and assumptions by themselves do not make Beethoven more revolutionary than they.

Moreover, each of Beethoven's works has many conventional features (that is, procedures followed by Haydn and Mozart and still adhered to by his contemporaries) and even conservative features (Haydnesque procedures that Beethoven's contemporaries had mostly abandoned). For Beethoven's first audience, these features of his music formed the background against which the unusual features played. In this sense, the conventional and conservative aspects of his pieces were indispensable to making the musical processes intelligible. An effort is required of modern listeners if they are to recover any of Beethoven's assumptions about what is foreground and what is background in his music. If the image of him as a revolutionary tempts us to suppose that this effort is unnecessary, it is mischievous. At the same time, however, the image of Beethoven as an innovator is somewhat justified by the fact that the set of features which are not unusual differs from one piece to the next. Although he was always conventional and conservative in some way, he was never conventional and conservative in the same way.

Whether or not the term "revolutionary" is appropriate for particular techniques in Beethoven's music or for his political ideas, the concept is relevant to thinking about the temporal processes projected by much of his music. It is relevant not so much because his temporal processes are revolutionarily innovative as because they are processes in which revolution or at least some understandings of revolution are viable concepts or because they are ambiguous in a way that makes one wonder whether revolution makes sense after all. To see this point one has only to compare and contrast Beethoven's to Haydn's and Mozart's sonata-allegro movements, even in the most general terms.

Beethoven's sonata-allegro movements resemble those of Haydn and Mozart in that they mirror the temporal process of a free agent shaping a future which responds both to the self and to the past. Like the composers of the high Classic period, Beethoven rejects the Newtonian assumption that a future is completely implicit in the present. Like theirs, his music is structured by the pairing of phrases and sections in which clearly articulated points of arrival both respond to what has prepared them and also suggest the fresh unexpectedness of a free agent's decision. The future is determined by both the past (which provides the context in which a free decision is made) and by the self (which makes a decision which is in principle less than completely predictable), and not by either alone. What comes to pass makes concrete and definite both the self and the goals toward which its past was tending. If a concept of revolution is to be viable, such concrete actualizations must be possible, at least in principle.

Still speaking generally, one can say that Beethoven's temporal processes differ from those of his predecessors in the degree to which he rejected the prevailing concepts of continuity, that is, his contemporaries' sense for what could appropriately follow what.[3] He risked discontinuity and followed pathways that were ambiguous and even tortured. Consequently, he enlarged the number of possible futures that the past and the self could evoke and shape. His music expanded its listeners' sense of what could follow a given past without falling into chaos. And his music prepared and arrived at events that were radically new in the sense that his predecessors could not and, without his achievements, his contemporaries would not have imagined them.

The newness of these arrivals and the extent to which they genuinely take place, as opposed to being merely adumbrated or fantasized, characterize a temporal process in which change can be profound and surprising. Yet the fulfillments in Beethoven's music are more significantly related to their past and to the self pressing toward them than are Haydn's and Mozart's points of arrival. More aspects of the past are consummated in the fulfillment. The sense of continuity is expanded and transformed. But unlike the mystical visionary, for whom fulfillment involves leaving temporality altogether, and unlike the apocalyptic seer, for whom the temporal process of which the past is the past is to be destroyed and a totally new one begun, Beethoven does not reject continuity.

The temporal processes in much of Beethoven's music are ones in which revolution is possible if "revolution" means actualizing a future that is not mechanically determined by the past and does not flow easily from human decisions, but that can be summoned only through a momentous struggle, yet is nevertheless profoundly related to the past. In many of his pieces, the wealth of unusual features makes continuity as well as fulfillment something that only an enormous exertion can achieve. The more the future has previously been unimagined and the more profoundly and comprehensively Beethoven seeks to relate the future to its past, the more violent is this struggle. Without such a struggle, continuity would evidently not be achieved, and events that are surprising would also seem arbitrary.

This sort of revolution comports with the self-understanding of those revolutionaries who see themselves as oriented toward a future in which some basic principle or essence will be fully manifest and who believe they are destroying the structures, established in the past, that presently inhibit that essence from controlling human experience. What is struggled against is presumed to be less appropriate to human nature than what is struggled for. Overcoming the impeding structures does not sever the future from the past, but in fact establishes the only kind of continuity that is worth establishing: the continuity of authentic human existence that in the past has been only incompletely actualized (because of inhibiting structures) with authentic human existence that in the future will be fully actualized (because the inimical structures will have been removed).

The possibility of revolution thus implies something about the nature and degree of change within the temporal process, something about the transformation of continuity and something about the struggle required to achieve significant change while maintaining continuity. These implications can be amplified and sharpened by considering several related issues. Three questions turn out to be particularly revealing. First, recognizing that the revolutionary chooses to orient himself toward the future, as opposed to living from the past, leads to the question, how does living toward the future affect one's experience of the present? Second, to what extent can the revolutionary's heroism, courage and self-sacrifice so stamp themselves on events that what becomes actual in the future will be congruent with the heroic self? And third, is it possible that free agents can integrate a variety of goals in the new future they are creating? These are, of course, questions that in one form or another have concerned philosophers from Plato to Theodor Adorno, and the common sense of each age has its responses to these problems, too.

Some of Beethoven's works suggest temporal processes in which the answers to these questions are surprisingly different from both the philosophical and the common-sense answers. Each of the following chapters will focus on one of these three questions and direct it to two of Beethoven's sonata-allegro movements. The temporal process exemplified by each movement — that is, the temporal process which can serve as a metaphor for the movement and for which the movement can serve as a metaphor — will be examined. In order to sharpen the descriptions of these temporal processes, each chapter will set two movements side by side and draw some comparisons; their temporal processes will be compared to each other, and the answers they offer for the chapter's focal question will be compared to some philosophical and common-sense approaches to the same issue. What follows is a quick overview:

A political or social event that might be called revolutionary differs, in part, from one that is not by the degree to which the deciding agent is oriented to the future as opposed to being oriented to the past. The two orientations are two different ways of experiencing the contrast between past, present and future. In both cases a decision occurs; the self and the past determine the future, and not either alone. But when the orientation is predominantly toward the past, the self lives from the conventions and goals set by previous events and makes no surprising decisions, while in the case of an orientation predominantly toward the future, the self lives toward the new arrivals it is trying to imagine and struggling to concretize. In the one, events look like the result of habits and routines, and what has already happened controls the feeling of moving toward the future. In the other, events seem unique, and what one hopes will take place affects the feeling of being alive in the present more than past events do. Chapter I will analyze the temporal process exemplified by the first movements of Beethoven's Trio in G, Op. 1, No. 2, and the String Quartet in F, Op. 59, No. 1. Each of these pieces in its own way presents both an image of living from the past and an image of living toward the future. The main business of the Trio is to transform a past-orientation into a future-orientation, while the Quartet presents a process in which the two apparently contradictory orientations become coincidental.

The risks and struggles that are involved in creating a radically new future come to the center of attention in chapter II, which analyzes the first movements of the "Archduke" Trio, Op. 97, and the "Hammerklavier" Sonata, Op. 106. The motifs and climaxes in both of these pieces have heroic connotations. In the first, heroism succeeds in establishing the future toward which it struggles. Likewise, in the second, magnificent and momentous gestures attain their goal, but the timing of its arrival is such that one realizes that this achievement has not obviated the need for other fulfillments. This realization seriously attenutes the sense that fulfillment has been actualized. A new future has taken place, but it is in some sense incongruent with the hero, and in that sense it is less than fulfilling.

Words like "decision," "heroism", and "revolution" suggest a singlemindedness that in fact characterizes very little of human experience. Most of the time all of us, including revolutionaries, are working toward a variety of goals on a variety of timetables. Some of these goals are mutually supportive; some of them are irrelevant to one another; some of them are mutually exclusive. The differences between our present experience and the experiences we expect or hope to have are so intricate and complex that we must ask whether the contrast between the present and the future is not only such that goals are realizable but also such that we can work simultaneously toward a variety of goals. Beethoven evidently sensed strongly that one may have a multiplicity of futures, and dared to write pieces in which discontinuity results from working toward two different futures at the same time. Chapter III will analyze two of these, the Piano Sonata in E Minor, Op. 90, in which two processes interweave and, in the end, confirm one another, and the String Quartet in A Minor, Op. 132, in which the ambiguity generated by two interwoven processes turns out to be irreducible and persistent.

In order to facilitate comparisons, works have been chosen that can all be said to be in sonata-allegro form and that all come from chamber music works. Analyzing only six movements — none of them representing Beethoven's other forms, none of them coming from his large-scale works (such as the Third Symphony and the Fifth Piano Concerto, whose heroic gestures make them obvious candidates for such a study), none of them placed in the context of the whole work from which it is taken — will not yield comprehensive results about his view of temporality.

Nevertheless, comparisons among only these six movements will suggest that he did not have a single view of the temporal process and that his images of temporality are complementary in some respects and contradictory in others. The six pieces are complementary in that all of them illustrate the way Beethoven's sonata-allegro movements are both similar to and different from Haydn's and Mozart's. On the one hand, their processes resemble the process of working toward goals that are determined by both their context and a self making a decision in that context; the six pieces are all images of striving to have such goals genuinely take place. On the other hand, all six pieces illustrate the way Beethoven risks more disruptive discontinuities, yet struggles to make the future even more continuous with the past than it is in Haydn and Mozart.

In some of the movements written after 1810, one finds temporal processes that are acutely incompatible. In these pieces Beethoven seems somewhat disillusioned with the assumptions that propelled sonata form in the 1780s. The mistimed arrival within the serious, heroic context of the Op. 106 Sonata and the tangle of threads within the Op. 90 Sonata and the Op. 132 Quartet show him trying to combine the assumptions about fulfillment and continuity with new ones. Other examples will emerge in chapters II and III. One might explain the incompatibilities among these images of temporality by regarding these movements as transitional to the Romantic style. One needs to keep in mind, however, that Beethoven's sonata-allegro forms never come as close to projecting a Romantic view of temporality as do some of his other forms.

In any case, the following chapters will not simply lump together the complementary aspects of these images by saying that they illustrate the way Beethoven is like and unlike Haydn an Mozart; nor will they simply lump together the contradictory aspects by saying that they illustrate the way Beethoven's music is transitional. Instead they will treat each movement as a unique entity and each image of temporality as a separate challenge to our view of temporality. The focal questions about revolution and temporality will serve as ways to approach each of these images and to develop metaphors for each movement's particular, distinctive quality. Although the questions are vitally important to understanding ourselves and our possibilities, no attempt will be made to deal with all of their ramifications nor to draw inferences from the answers Beethoven's images seem to suggest. Consequently, the six analyses do not march to a conclusion about the temporal process in Beethoven's music nor about his final attitude toward revolution nor even about changes in his understanding of temporality. They do form a progression, however, in the sense that later sections, dealing with pieces that listeners have always found difficult to understand, are enriched by using concepts developed in earlier sections and by drawing comparisons that may clarify the more complex images.

Although each of the six movements is a unique entity, each is also an example of a style shared by Beethoven with contemporaneous composers who were likewise imitating and extending Haydn's and Mozart's styles. The obvious fact that Beethoven's musical language was not entirely of his own making makes it useful to compare his practice with that of his contemporaries by identifying those aspects of each piece that are unusual and seldom occur in pieces by other composers and those that occur frequently in pieces by others. Each Beethoven movement (like all good music) has a set of usual and unusual features that is peculiar to it; it is not the case that the same set of unusual features is to be found in all of Beethoven's pieces or even in all of the pieces from the same period of his life. Identifying a movement's peculiar set of usual and unusual features gives a clue — though not an infallible key — to what makes it unique and endows it with a particular, distinguishing quality. Knowing a movement's unusual aspects leads one to ask how these features interact with each other and how each is justified by the total context supplied by other (usual and unusual) aspects of the movement. Moreover, knowing that a feature is unusual confirms that it really is salient to the movement's uniqueness: the judgment that the movement is truly distinctive implies that among its salient features are at least some that are not shared by a large number of undistinguished pieces. At the same time, the judgment that it is in roughly the same style as these other pieces implies that it shares many features with them and that the shared features create the background against which the salient features appear.

In order to compare Beethoven to his contemporaries, a study was made of 238 randomly selected sonata-allegro movements written by lesser known composers and published in Vienna between 1795 and 1826 (see Appendix). Approximately 2800 pieces with at least one movement in sonata form were published in Vienna during these years, and 238 is a sufficiently large percentage of these to permit the assumption that the features occurring in these 238 movements can be found with about the same frequency in the others.[4] Of the 238, 50 were published between 1795 and 1800 (the period during which Beethoven's Op. 1 Trios were published), 61 between 1801 and 1808 (the period of the Op. 59 Quartets), 43 between 1809 and 1814 (the period of the "Archduke" and the Op. 90 Sonata), 55 between 1815 and 1823 (the period of the "Hammerklavier") and 29 between 1824 and 1826 (the period of the Op. 132 Quartet). The study of the 238 movements consisted of identifying many of the decisions a composer made in writing a sonata-allegro movement, as well as the alternative choices available for each decision, and then counting the number of times each alternative appeared. Using these data, one can identify the unusual features in a Beethoven movement as those that occur infrequently in contemporaneous works. This information will be used in the following chapters as only one way among others to confirm that a particular feature is indeed striking and to lead to the question, what role does it play in the movement?[5]

The analyses that follow are by no means complete descriptions. Many interesting details of each movement are passed over. Mention is made primarily of those aspects that pertain to the temporal process exemplified by the movement and especially to the issues associated with the struggle for both revolutionary change and underlying continuity. Each analysis presupposes a particular way of hearing the movement, and enough other aspects are mentioned to let the reader know what that hearing is and to justify this way as at least a possible one. Music analysts, of course, always hope that their way of hearing a piece is not only a possible one but is also the best one in the sense that it encompasses all the aspects of the piece and exhibits their interrelation such that the music itself is as coherent as possible. But the criteria of coherence vary from one analyst to the next, and often this variation is a function of different, unconsciously held presuppositions about the nature of the temporal process. In the following chapters, the analysis of each particular movement attempts to let that movement's view of temporality come to the surface even if this view flies in the face of common sense and makes the piece, judged by some cannons of common sense, incoherent.

Notes

1. But see Maynard Soloman, *Beethoven* (1977), p. 64.

2. These facts emerged from a study of 238 sonata-allegro movements written by Beethoven's contemporaries and published in Vienna between 1795 and 1826. These movements are listed in the Appendix. This investigation was supported by a grant from the American Philosophical Society.

For examples, see Adalbert Gyrowetz's String Quartet in A Major, Op. 21/1/i (1798), in which the second theme is in the subdominant, or his String Quartet in E-flat Major, Op. 29/1/i (1799–1800), in which the second theme is in C major; Joseph Wölfl's Sonata in C Major, Op. 2/1/i (1796), in which there is no caesura between the bridge and the set of paired phrases in the dominant and hence the onset of the second theme is obscure; and Josef Eybler's Sonata in C Minor (1798), in which the exposition is not repeated.

3. Jonathan D. Kramer, "Multiple and Non-linear Time in Beethoven's Opus 135," *Perspectives of New Music*, vol. 11 (1973), pp. 122–45, suggests that Beethoven could even make the future take place before the past that prepares it and to which it responds has occurred!

4. The number 2800 is reached by using Alexander Weinmann's lists of the music published by Viennese publishing houses and counting those pieces whose titles suggest that they have at least one movement in sonata-allegro form. The information needed for a precise count is not available, and the following necessarily arbitrary decisions were made in arriving at the number 2800: (1) Lists of the works published by the Chemische Druckerei, P. Cappi, Pennauer, Sauer and Weigl are not yet available; we do know, however, the total output of these firms during the years 1795–1826, and assuming they published pieces with a sonata-allegro movement about as frequently as other houses generates an approximate figure. (2) In many cases it is impossible to determine from a work's title whether it contains a sonata movement; nevertheless, pieces identified as a duet, duo, trio, duo concertante, trio concerante and sonatina are included in the count (though one finds instances of works under all these titles that have no sonata movement, and it is impossible to verify the presence of a sonata movement in cases where the music itself is no longer extant); pieces identified as divertimenti and serenades are excluded from the count (though one finds some instances of works under these titles that do have a sonata movement). (3) It is sometimes impossible to determine from a title whether the piece is a vocal or instrumental duet or trio, and these pieces are omitted from the count. (4) Pieces which are published more than once by the same or different firms are counted at each appearance, provided a new plate was used for each new edition. (5) But works whose plates were bought by a second publisher who issued copies struck from these plates under his own name are not counted twice. (6) Weinmann bases his lists on publishers' notices in newspapers; sometimes a publisher's notice would indicate a set of three quartets, while in fact he published only one of the three; in the cases when the music is not extant, it is not always possible to verify the publisher's number, but nevertheless, it is used in making the count.

The titles of Weinmann's books on which the count of sonata-allegro movements is based follow: *Verlagsverzeichnis Giovanni Cappi bis A.O. Witzendorf* (1967); *Verlagsverzeichnis Pietro Machetti quondem Carlo* (1966); *Verlagsverzeichnis Tranquillo Mollo* (1964); *Verzeichnis der Musikalien aus dem K.K. Hoftheater-Musik-Verlage* (1963); *Verzeichnis der Musikalien des Verlages Johann Traeg in Wien 1794–1818* from *Studien zur Musikwissenschaft*, vol. 23 (1956); *Verzeichnis der Musikalien des Verlages Joseph Eder-Jeremias Berman* (1966); *Verzeichnis der Verlagswerke des Musikalischen Magazins in Wien, 1784–1802, "Leopold Kozeluch"* (1950); *Vollständiges Verlagsverzeichnis Artaria & Comp.* (1952); *Vollständiges Verlagsverzeichnis der Musikalien des Kunst- und Industrie Comptoirs in Wien 1801–19* from *Studien zur Musikwissenschaft* vol. 20 (1955); *Wiener Musikverlage "am Rande"* (1970); *Wiener Musikverleger und Musikalienhändler von Mozarts Zeit bis gegen 1860* (1956); *Die Wiener Verlagswerke von Franz Anton Hoffmeister* (1964).

5. Rosen, *op. cit.*, p. 32, points out that some pieces by some composers exert more influence than do others, and thus arriving at a sense of the style, against which certain features are unusual or striking, by choosing pieces randomly is to be more democratic than realistic. Certainly the sense of the style of the 1795–1826 sonata movements expressed as a series of the frequencies with which alternative decisions appear has no priority over the sense one develops from a creative synthesis of a large number of pieces in which frequency of performance and lines of influence are kept in mind. But the former approach may lead to observations and thence to questions that even the latter may find interesting.

CHAPTER I

Living from the Past/
Living toward the Future

---

1. Trio in G, Op. 1, No. 2, First Movement

(1) Front-heaviness

WHEN WE listen to music, we are usually most explicitly aware of the melodic and rhythmic motifs, the prominent cadences and any unusually colorful turns in the harmony. On reflection we realize that we have also been affected by the underlying harmony and by the interaction between the harmony and the change or reprise of melodic ideas. We are seldom explicitly aware of the proportions of the movement — the length of one section compared to the length of another. Yet these proportions have an important effect on the musical experience. The proportions of Beethoven's G Major Trio, Op. 1/2/i (1795), are extraordinary. We can see how unusual they are by comparing them to the relative lengths of corresponding sections in other sonata-allegro movements published in Vienna between 1795 and 1800. The data are:

    1) The first part of the first theme (i.e. the music from the beginning of the first phrase in the Allegro Vivace to the beginning of the phrase paired to it; bars 28–50) is 1.44 times longer than the second part of the first theme (the paired phrase; bars 51–66). This ratio is larger in Beethoven's Op. 1/2/i than it is in 88% of his contemporaries' sonata-allegro movements.

61

2) The first theme paired phrases (bars 28–66) are 1.77 times longer than the second theme paired phrases (bars 100–121). The extent by which the length of Beethoven's first theme surpasses that of the second theme is greater than in 94% of the other 1795–1800 movements.

3) Beethoven's first theme is 28% of the whole exposition (bars 28–166). More of his exposition is occupied by the first theme than is the case in 72% of the other 1795–1800 expositions.

4) Because Beethoven's bridge (bars 67–99) is also comparatively short, the first part of his exposition (first theme plus bridge) is 1.07 times longer than the second part (second theme plus exposition closing). In only 6% of the contemporary movements is the first part of the exposition such a large proportion of the whole.

5) In Beethoven's recapitulation, the ratio of the first-theme-plus-bridge(bars 252–320) to the second-theme-plus-closing (bars 321–97) is 0.90. This ratio is larger than the corresponding ratio in 82% of the other 1795–1800 recapitulations. In other words, even though the second half of Beethoven's recapitulation (excluding the coda) is a little longer than the first part, it is not nearly as much longer as the corresponding sections of most contemporary recapitulations are.

6) In Beethoven's Trio, the exposition plus its repeat is 120% of the length of the development plus recapitulation (excluding the coda).

All these data show a pronounced front-heaviness: either in absolute terms or relative to other movements or both, the first part of a section is significantly longer than the second part to which it is paired or linked. A front-heavy section sounds clumsy and wobbly. When an event that is prepared is conspicuously less weighty than the event preparing it, the sense of arrival is seriously attenuated. The shorter passage is not an adequate fulfillment. One feels that, although what has been prepared has in some sense been concretized, nevertheless some further actualization would be appropriate. Front-heaviness is a stout brand of instability. The fact that front-heaviness is found so rarely and never so pervasively in the music of Beethoven's contemporaries confirms the sense one has in listening to this movement that its proportions are somehow discordant with its Classical style.

Front-heaviness significantly affects the metaphor that the movement creates for the temporal process. Understanding this effect requires that one recognize first the factors that generate front-heaviness and then the way that Beethoven in the end provides the fulfillment which the front-heavy groups lack.

(2) Features Generating Front-heaviness: the Ambiguity of Continuing and Beginning

The front-heaviness of Beethoven's movement does not sound arbitrary, for it is related to other features, each of which has its own justification.

The process resulting in front-heaviness begins with the twenty-seven-measure slow introduction that precedes the exposition. The function of a slow introduction is to define the musical space in which the rest of the movement will move. That is, it sets forth the register in which the main musical events will happen, the tonal center of that register, and the timbre of sounds articulating that center. If there were no slow introduction, the paired phrases of the first theme would have to open up the musical space as well as to establish the movement's main melodic and rhythmic materials. In the Trio, Op. 1/2/i, the register, range, timbre and tonality are defined before the melodic motifs are clearly specified. Although the motifs that will come in the Allegro Vivace are anticipated and adumbrated in the slow introduction (e.g. bar 24), it is melodically vague. But because it defines the other parameters of the musical space, it allows the first theme a degree of melodic freedom it could not have if it had to open up the movement's space.

Beethoven (or his theme) exercises this freedom by beginning not on the tonic but by extending the dominant harmony, on which the introduction ends, for five measures. Had there been no introduction, the first phrase would not have been able to delay the tonic so long without ceasing to be a phrase, that is, a gesture that is in some sense stable at the same time that it is unstable enough to generate a pair. It is, in fact, incorrect to say that the introduction "ends", for there is no closure separating it from the first theme. The first theme starts with a single voice (piano) that simply continues the single thread of the last two bars of the introduction. There is no sense of the Allegro beginning; one does not hear the onset of a phrase moving towards a paired phrase. Instead, after a few measures, one has the sense of "having begun."

FIGURE 11

Beethoven, Trio in G for Violin, Cello and Piano, Op. 1, No. 2, first movement

FIGURE 12

First way of hearing bars 28—43:

4+4	4+4	(Curved lines
28—35	36—43	above numbers indi-
ante-	conse-	cate motivic
cedent	quent	similarities.)

Second way of hearing bars 28—43:

2+2	2+2	2+2	2+2
28—31	32—35	36—39	40—43
ante.	cons.	ante.	cons.

antecedent	consequent

Another way to describe the opening of the Allegro Vivace is to say that it modulates the contrast between continuing one thing and beginning a new thing. In the common-sense view of temporality, these two are mutually exclusive, yet Beethoven presents a process that falls exactly in between them. And as measures 28–43 (quoted in Figure 11) unfold, various other moments also modulate this contrast and seem to be as much a continuing as a beginning. These measures group themselves in two different ways. First, one hears bars 28–43 as a single phrase consisting of a pair of eight-bar subphrases (28–35 and 36–43). Each subphrase is divided into two equal parts; the ceasuras that we hear in bars 31 and 39 are not clear cadences, but are analogous to the non-cadential articulations that divide subphrases into two equal parts in most Classic-period paired phrases (compare what happens in bars 31 and 39 to what happens at the end of bar 2 and in the middle of bar 7 of "Eine kleine Nachtmusik," Figure 3). But, second, one also hears bars 28–43 as analogous to a pair of phrases, each phrase consisting of a pair of four-bar subphrases, as though there were cadences in bars 31 and 39 after all. Two aspects of the music imply this grouping: while the divisions in bars 31 and 39 are not clear cadences, they sound enough like the close of a group to suggest that 28–31 is a subphrase paired to 32–35 and that 36–39 is a subphrase paired to 40–43. And each of these four-bar groups is internally divided into two symmetrical two-bar groups. The diagram in Figure 12 sketches both ways of hearing these sixteen measures.

One hears these two different and apparently mutually exclusive groupings of bars 28–43 because what happens in bars 31 and 39 is analogous both to the articulation dividing a subphrase into two symmetrical parts and to the cadence closing a subphrase. Each of these two caesuras modulates the contrast between an articulation within a subphrase and an articulation ending a subphrase. And so bars 32 and 40 modulate the contrast between the continuation of a subphrase (an eight-bar subphrase) and the beginning of a new four-bar subphrase. Because bars 32 and 40 sound like both a continuation and a beginning, listeners do not know when they hear the decisive close in bar 43 whether they have heard a pair of eight-bar subphrases and can expect another pair, or whether they have heard a pair of eight-bar phrases, each with a pair of four-bar subphrases. And so bar 43 also modulates the contrast between continuing (according to the first hearing, bar 43 launches the continuation of the first theme) and beginning (according to the second hearing, bar 43 ends the first theme and launches the beginning of something new).

Measures 51–66 work in favor of the first hearing, for here we get a sixteen-bar phrase that is clearly paired to measures 28–43. But before the paired phrase announces itself, the tonic harmony ending the first phrase is prolonged for seven measures. The seven-bar prolongation is generated by the character of the first phrase — that is, by the very same features that modulate the contrast between continuing and beginning. With all its symmetrical divisions, subdivisions and subdivisions of its subdivisions, the first phrase is so highly organized that it builds up pressure for more fluent motion. Propelled by this pressure, the seven-bar prolongation with its written-in accelerando (especially bars 43, 45 and 47) bursts the confines of excessive structure. (The relation of the highly structured first phrase to the fluent seven-bar prolongation closely resembles the bond tying a taut paired phrase structure to a fluent bridge, a bond commonly found in Classic sonata-allegro movements and illustrated in part 2, section (1), subsection (i) of this chapter by a Gyrowetz sonata.)

Because these seven measures extend the cadence ending the first phrase, they belong to the first phrase and make it longer than the second. The front-heaviness that will pervade most of the movement is established. In that these seven measures are generated by the very features that modulate the contrast between continuing and beginning in the first theme, the connection between front-heaviness and modulated contrast is audible and tight.

Absolutely critical to the temporal process projected by the movement as a whole, this connection is by no means accidental. By its very nature, a gesture that seems both to prolong a preparatory gesture and to begin a new one that would actualize what has been prepared almost has to engender front-heaviness. Such a gesture makes the listener sense that the fulfilling event does not quite take shape. So long as the ambiguity persists, the listener must feel that what has happened so controls what is happening that the latter is more a continuation of the past than the arrival of a distinctive, fulfilling future. The upshot of this process is that when the distinctive future does arrive, it is overbalanced by its weightier past. To say that the first theme as a whole is front-heavy is to say that the arrival connoted by the onset of the second phrase (bar 51) is more dominated by its past than the past was oriented toward its future. It is fitting that this second phrase, like its pair, has four-bar units that both do and do not function as subphrases.

The process of ambiguously continuing while beginning also interacts with front-heaviness during the second theme. The caesura in bar 99 articulating the end of the bridge and the beginning of the second theme is the strongest thus far in the movement. Moreover, the bridge is so long that it discharges most of the energy developed by the modulation from G to D, and the only forward thrust from the bridge into the second theme is the push generated by the new key's dominant which prevails from bar 93 to its brief resolution in bar 99. Consequently, the beginning of the second theme sounds somewhat like a new beginning to the movement — another first theme as it were.

After four bars of the second theme, but not until then, the listener may realize that the second theme has the same melodic skeleton as the first theme (see Figure 13). The second phrase, which starts at the end of bar 113, borrows more overtly from the first theme. About half of the second themes in the sonata movements of 1795–1800 borrow motifs from their first themes, and the procedure helps unify the musical flow. Although Beethoven's use of the same melodic skeleton is unusual and subtle, his procedure, like his contemporaries', establishes continuity and counteracts the absence of note-to-note notion at the end of the bridge and the absence of strong forward thrust from the bridge.

FIGURE 13

The second theme, by the time it is over, sounds paired to the first theme because it is more stable than the first theme in at least six respects: the second theme seems more predictable and less nervous because its flow is more continuous and it has less rhythmic variety; the anacruses to its subphrases give them a firm footing, while the absence of upbeats in the first theme makes it sound as though it were tumbling forward somewhat out of control; the second theme is end-heavy (bars 122–40 prolong the final cadence and make the second phrase considerably longer than the first); the motion from the first phrase to its pair is more fluent in the second theme than in the first (although there is a clear break in bar 113, it has neither the sense of return after a completed gesture nor the contrasting dynamic levels that characterize bar 50); and the second theme has none of the first theme's ambiguity about its four-measure units (in the second theme these groups are clearly subphrases). All these stabilizing features occur more often in the second theme than in the first in the other 1795-1800 sonata movements, but rarely do so many of them appear in the same second theme. Relative to contemporary practice, Beethoven is exaggerating the stability of his second theme. The more stable it is, compared the first theme, the more strongly it is paired to the comparatively mobile first theme. The force of this bond pulls the exposition as a whole into a single section in spite of the lack of note-to-note continuity at the beginning of the second theme and the fairly weak thrust into it from the bridge.

In the first theme, one is more aware of continuity than of change at the points where something new begins. In fact, it is only retrospectively that one realizes that something has in fact begun. In the second theme, the ambiguity works the other way around: at first one is aware of discontinuity and of a new beginning; only after four bars is one aware of the melodic similarity linking the themes, and only at the end of the second theme does the listener known how effectively its stability pairs it to the first theme.

Because its discontinuity is more immediately conspicuous, the onset of the second theme cannot function as a point of arrival. And although its exaggerated stability pairs it to the first theme, it is the briefer of the two. Consequently, the exposition as a whole has an awkward, front-heavy shape in which no event takes place that would serve as an image of the tendencies of a past reaching their destination. Front-heaviness and non-arrival reinforce one another's effects, and the listener may well feel at the end of the exposition that the movement into the future has been oriented toward the past. This feeling is further supported by the way the exposition closing (upbeat to bar 141 through bar 166) alludes to the first theme. The rhythm of the opening motif (♩♫ ; see bars 144, 146, 151, 161, 162) and its melody (compare bars 145, 162, 163 to bar 29) pervade the exposition closing. In some exposition closings, the restatement of the opening motif is heard as the destination toward which the bridge and second theme are heading. There is no sense of such a return here, for in spite of the apparent new beginning at the onset of the second theme, the first theme was never decisively left. Instead of hearing a departure during the bridge and the second theme, and return at the exposition closing, the listener feels simply that what has already happened is what is continuing to happen.[1]

It is, of course, continuing to happen in a new key. The harmonic contrast between the two parts of the exposition projects a kind of departure, and in the recapitulation the reestablishment of the tonic and the reprise of melodic material project a sense of return. But this feeling of return is seriously attenuated by three features that keep the recapitulation from sounding like a climactic point of arrival: the nature of the development, the brevity of the retransition and the character of the first theme itself. The conspicuous breaks in the development (bars 190 and 234) divide it into two sections plus a retransition. Each of the two sections is about as long as each of the four sections of the exposition. Moreover, the allusions to exposition material are always explicit, and the first theme's motif is pervasive. In short, the development does not have the unstable structural or motivic vagueness that in most developments press toward the return of stable, definite gestures at the recapitulation.

The retransition (bars 234–51) is not unusually long (44% of the other 1795-1800 retransitions are a larger proportion of the whole development). Its prolongation of the dominant builds up pressure towards a tonic, but not very strong pressure.

The reprise of the first theme — beginning as it does on the fourth degree of the scale over an implied dominant harmony — overlaps the end of the retransition. Like the joint between the end of the slow introduction and the start of the exposition, this joint is disguised. The recapitulation is underway before it has clearly begun.

The climax that comes at the beginning of the recapitulation in many of the contemporary sonata movements occurs at the beginning of the second phrase (bar 267) in Beethoven's recapitulation. Because measures 44–50 are not recapitulated, the climax is not delayed unduly. Moreover, this abbreviation removes the front-heaviness that characterizes the exposition's first theme. Because the recapitulation bridge is also a shortened version of its exposition counterpart while there is no abbreviation in the reprise of the second theme, the front-heaviness that marks the exposition is eased, although it is not removed.

(3) Front-heaviness Changing into End-heaviness

The recapitulation ends with a decisive closure in bar 397. Because the front-heaviness within the exposition and the front-heaviness of the exposition relative to the rest of the movement have not yet been removed, the movement sounds unfinished in spite of the resounding cadence. The front-heaviness propels a long coda.

The coda, like the bridge, the exposition closing, the development and the recapitulation begins with the first theme's rhythmic motif (♩♫). But this restatement, unlike those, sounds like a genuine return: it is squarely in the tonic and its beginning, although soft, is decisive and unambiguous.

Beethoven's coda is long; only 4% of the 1795–1800 movements have a coda that is longer relative to the whole movement. It is, in fact, so long that it transforms the shape of the movement from front-heavy to end-heavy. The ratio of the development-plus-recapitulation-plus-coda to the introduction-plus-exposition-plus-exposition-repeat is larger than the corresponding ratio in 76% of the 1795–1800 movements.

Before the coda, the proportions of Beethoven's movement suggest the metaphor of a temporal process in which one's past seems weightier and more controls the present texture and quality of existence than are and do current circumstances and possibilities. It is a temporality in which one is so preoccupied with what has happened, whether pleasant or unpleasant, that coming events, even those that are certain or desirable, touch only lightly how it feels to be alive at the present. The coda transforms the movement as a whole into an image of temporal experience in which anticipating or living toward a future, whether desired or dreaded, contributes more than anything else to the way the present feels.

The front-heaviness that prevails before the coda results largely from the several instances in which the beginning of a new part sounds more like the continuation of the previous part than a genuine change. Not only does this ambiguity engender the front-heaviness that suggests a past-orientation, but it also is itself an image of living predominantly from the past. At the start of both the exposition and the recapitulation and at the start of the second, third and fourth four-bar units in both the exposition and recapitulation, the arrival of the prepared event is somewhat disguised so that it sounds like a continuation of what has already been heard. These gestures suggest the sort of change that must be attributed to the decision of a self that is free (a new section does begin, as the listener recognizes a few bars later, and so the past does not seem to determine the future mechanically), but that is mostly past-oriented; in the process of change projected by these moments, living from the past masks the arrival of what is new (change is experienced, initially at least, as mere continuation). In short, these gestures are the image of a process in which a free self decides to continue what has been happening and to repeat the past's patterns.

A past-oriented decision must be distinguished from the unfolding of a necessity. When the analogy to nature's process of cause and effect holds, the implications of the past completely control the future. Both past- and future-oriented decisions differ from the unfolding of a necessity, because in both cases what happens cannot be exhaustively explained by referring to the past. To say that the music is an image of living from the past is to make a comment on how the change is understood by the agent and how experiencing it feels; it is not to impugn the genuineness of the decision. In a past-oriented decision, one is free and takes responsibility for the decision, but what one opts for is always what is familiar and as much as possible a repetition of past routines and patterns. It is a decision to be conventional. In it, one seeks to maximize the similarities between oneself and other selves, and to actualize oneself through continuing established patterns. One aims to do what any unparticularized self would do in the given circumstances. This sort of self-actualization is inadequate to the uniqueness of each self. Sensing this inadequacy makes the outcome of one's past-oriented decisions seem less than completely fulfilling even if what comes to pass is more surprising and less a continuation of the past than one bargained for. A past-oriented decision may have unconventional outcomes without feeling less conventional to the agent. The obverse is also true: self-conscious revolutionaries make future-oriented decisions, and they intend that their outcome be a break with habitual practices, but the actual outcome may superficially look routine; yet the decision itself may still exemplify living toward the future.

Just as the coda as a whole transforms a process that has consistently been front-heavy into an end-heavy one, and to hear the movement is to experience a past-orientation turn into a future-orientation, so also the onset of the coda is the image of a future-oriented decision. This moment begins transforming an image of living from the past into an image of living toward the future. To a certain extent, the coda is justified by the unstable front-heaviness that has characterized the movement up to this point, but one cannot say that the front-heaviness literally forces the transformation to take place. The coda seems warranted, but not literally necessary. It does not suggest a process in which the past determines the future, but a process in which the past and a free self together shape the future. The beginning of the coda is prepared, yet surprising. Because it deals effectively with the instability created by the front-heaviness of the movement up to that point, it can be siad to be genuinely responsive to its past. Because its beginning is clearly demarcated, it is a decisive moment — an eventful occurrence, not merely a continuation of the past.

In this sense, then, the transformation is an image of revolutionary change. Like a revolution, the transformation is an eventful occurrence that is utterly mysterious from the perspective in which the future is seen as the necessary unfolding of the past (and in which the concept of "decision" is nonsense) and that is utterly bewildering from the perspective in which the freely made choice to uphold habits established in the past is always regarded as the best decision.

Although the rhythmic motif at the beginning and indeed all the material throughout the course of the coda is derived from earlier parts of the movement, the passage is fresh and exciting. The connotations of the rhythmic motif are radically changed. At the onset of the exposition and the recapitulation, this motif associates itself with the ambiguity of beginning while continuing, hence with a past-orientation. Here, at the coda, it unequivocally connotes a future-oriented goal-directedness: it itself thrusts to its own completion, and because the coda resolves the tension generated by the movement's front-heavy groupings, it functions as the goal of the whole movement. The use of familiar material suggests that the new future-oriented subject is in some sense continuous with the formerly past-oriented subject, and that in outward respects its world is largely the same. It does not suggest that the decision to live toward the future instead of from the past is a past-oriented decision, for regardless of the familiarity of the material, the transformation itself sounds unfamiliar and the new orientation feels strange. To undergo the transformation of an orientation primarily toward the past into an orientation primarily toward the future is to experience as fundamental a change as any through which a person can pass.

2. String Quartet in F, Op. 59, No. 1, First Movement

Those who reject a past-oriented temporality generally do so because they do not want to cut themselves off from new possibilities. Whether or not they condemn the past, they choose, or find themselves in, a temporal process where hitherto unknown events are realizable and desirable. The opposite kind of rejection — the choice not to live toward the future — is prompted by one of two reasons. Some past-oriented people choose, or find themselves in, a temporal process in which they do not expect the future, when it takes place, to be genuinely new or, if they do anticipate some change, do not expect to evaluate the novel occurrence positively; this is the conservative rejection of a future-orientation. Others who reject a future-orientation live a temporality in which the arrival of the new possibility is either the end of the temporal process, in the sense that one is oriented toward an atemporal reality and no longer to a concretely realizable future (the "*Liebestod*" in *Tristan* symbolizes such an orientation), or the arrival is never a final fulfillment that would obviate the need for a further fulfillment; this is the Romantic rejection of a future-orientation.

The opening movement of Beethoven's String Quartet, Op. 59, No. 1 (1806), is, up to the coda, as relentlessly future-oriented as the Op. 1/2 Trio movement, up to its coda, is past-oriented. While the Trio transforms front-heaviness into end-heaviness and a past-orientation into a future-orientation, the Quartet does not make the opposite kind of move. Instead, by its end, it has so synthesized living from the past and living toward the future that the reasons for rejecting one and choosing the other lose their force. While the transformation in Op. 1/2/i of a past-orientation into a future-orientation is an image of revolutionary change, the synthesis in Op. 59/1/i of the two orientations undercuts the revolutionaries' insistence that only an orientation toward what ought to be is appropriate to the contrast they feel between what is and what ought to be. If the radical difference between living from the past and living toward the future disappears, then the point of distinguishing revolutionary change and continuity from other kinds of change and continuity and then holding firmly to the former also disappears.

(1) Images of Living toward the Future

The key to feeling the powerful pull of the future in Op. 59/1/i is recognizing the shape of the first theme, of the exposition as a whole, and of the movement as a whole and then realizing that these three shapes are identical. The key to hearing this shape is to notice the discrepancy between the places where the note-to-note continuity is broken and the places where new sections begin.

In the sonata forms of Beethoven's predecessors and contemporaries, the points where the flow halts usually coincide with the points where change occurs, and it is precisely these coincidences that create the identifiable entities or sections that are analogous to one another in the various and varied sonata-allegro movements. Using the names that have emerged to call attention to these analogies, one can refer to these points as the beginning of the bridge, the beginning of the second theme, the beginning of the development and the beginning of the recapitulation. In Op. 59/1ii Beethoven gives his listeners clues enough to assure them that they are hearing a sonata-form movement. Yet he deviates from the expectations the form implies by putting strong caesuras in the middle of the first theme (bar 19) and the bridge (bar 48; see Figure 14), while the note-to-note continuity elsewhere in the exposition is so strong that one does not hear articulated sections that could be identified as a bridge or as an exposition closing. What is unusual is not that there are no articulations that would mark the beginning of the bridge or the closing but that elsewhere there are strong articulations that do not mark the beginning of sections. It is even more remarkable that the note-to-note motion is so continuous that the onset of the second theme (bar 60) is somewhat obscured. Beethoven also departs from sonata-form conventions by marking articulations within the development (at bars 126 and 144) more clearly than those at either the beginning or the end of the development.

(i) The Exposition

In spite of the caesura within the bridge and the lack of one at its end, the attentive listener notices the beginning of the second theme. In bar 60, transition-like material is clearly replaced by themelike material. The second theme is a point of arrival. It is the image of a moment when one has gotten to where one was heading, for in it the sense of driving forward, while not completely absent, is considerably relaxed. The second theme turns out the be much stabler than the first theme: it has less rhythmic variety, less skipwise motion, fewer subphrases beginning without an anacrusis, longer upbeats to subphrases, less sequential motion and more continuous motion (because the non-cadential articulations within the subphrases are weaker in the second theme). The thetic quality of the second theme relative to the first enhances the sense of arrival at the second theme, and makes it an identifiable entity in spite of the way its beginning overlaps the end of the bridge.

FIGURE 14
Beethoven, String Quartet in F, Op. 59, No. 1, first movement

The sense of arrival in bar 60 is not, however, the first one experienced in the movement. In bar 39, the appearance of B-natural signals a change of tonal center and the arrival of a new section. But the sense of arrival in bar 39 is attenuated by two factors. First, the B-natural and the dominant of the dominant it implies are anticipated in bars 25 and 26. At those earlier points, F is reinstated as a tonic at once, and one cannot be sure in bar 39 that F will not reappear again. Second, there is little contrast between the degree to which bars 1–38 are structured and the tightness of the structure in bars 39–59. Although rhythmically and melodically bars 1–4 form a unit, no cadence closes this group. It is somewhat like a subphrase paired to bars 5–19, but only somewhat. Bar 19 has a strong closure on the tonic. Bars 1–19 act as a first phrase paired to a second phrase only because this cadence is prolonged by transitional material (bars 20–29) that builds pressure toward a second phrase (bars 30–38). Bars 30–31 are a variation of bars 2–3, and this melodic echo together with the instability generated by bars 20–29 make bars 30–38 a loose analogue to a consequent phrase. In short, bars 1–38 are structured into paired groups, though weakly, while there is no pairing within bars 39–59. Thus, one hears a contrast, though a mild one, between 1–38 and 39–59, a contrast that is confirmed by the written-in accelerando of bars 42–43 and 46–50. The differences between what happens before and what happens after the B-natural in bar 39 are great enough that one senses the beginning of a new section at this point, an occurrence that has been prepared by and that flows out of the previous section.

The sense in which the first theme (bars 1–38) prepares bars 39–59 can be clarified by comparing the former to the large number of contemporary first themes that are highly organized and that end with a decisive cadence. They consist of a pair of phrases, each comprising a pair of subphrases, and each subphrase being divided by a non-cadential articulation into two balancing parts. The very fact that the musical flow has been channeled into such highly organized parts creates pressure to burst out of the confines of such structure, and the subsequent section, with its characteristic written-in accelerando, relieves this pressure. When the responding section is also melodically or harmonically transitional to a set of paired phrases in a new key, it is appropriately called a bridge. Alternating paired with non-paired material makes the former create a pair with the latter; the process is an important and typical method for achieving higher-level coherence in these works.

Figure 16, quoting the beginning to Gyrowetz's Sonata for Piano with Violin and Cello Obbligato, Op. 34/1/i (1801), illustrates this

FIGURE 15*

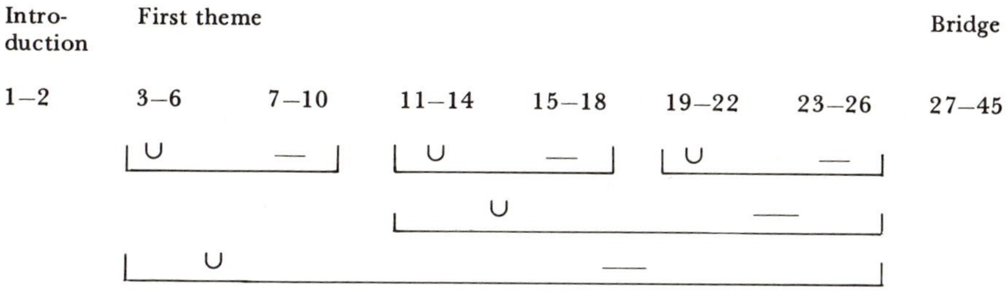

Intro- duction	First theme							Bridge
1–2	3–6	7–10	11–14	15–18	19–22	23–26	27–45

process. Gyrowetz gives us two introductory bars, then three phrases, each phrase consisting of a pair of subphrases, and each subphrase consisting of two symmetrical subunits. The three phrases form the pairs sketched in Figure 15. With the upbeat to bar 27, the music finally bursts out of this tight, intensively organized structure. The moment of release is such a strong point of arrival that bars 27–45 form a pair with bars 3–26.

Bars 1–38 of Beethoven's Op. 59/1/i are organized intensively enough to make them analogous to his contemporaries' first themes. The more fluent passage (bars 39ff.) does seem prepared by and responsive to the more structured passage (bars 1–38), though the sense of moving from preparation to fulfillment is considerably weaker here than in gestures like bars 3–45 of the Gyrowetz Sonata or bars 28–51 of Beethoven's Trio, Op. 1/2/i.

Beethoven's bars 38ff. seem to be generated particularly by bars 30–38. Bar 34 seems to end a lower-level antecedent group because its melody ends on the comparatively unstable third degree of the scale. The answering subphrase begins with identical melodic material, and one expects it to be a consequent subphrase; yet its ending is also

* In this and other sketches, bar numbers refer to the first and last downbeats of a section. Thus, the first theme is shown as beginning in bar 3, even though the last two and a half beats of bar 26 are part of the bridge. The same bar number is used for the last bar of one section and the first bar of the next only when the ending of a section so overlaps the beginning of the next that the downbeat of the bar functions in both sections.

Following the practice used in Grosvenor Cooper and Leonard Meyer, *The Rhythmic Structure of Music* (1960), these sketches use a breve (∪) to indicate that a musical gesture (a bar, a measure, a phrase or a section) is analogous to an anacrusis in poetry and a macron (—) to indicate a musical gesture that has a thetic quality.

FIGURE 16
Adalbert Gyrowetz, Sonata in F for Piano with Violin and Cello Obbligato, Op. 34,
No. 1, first movement

identical — its melody also ends on the unstable third degree — and so one hears its extension (the last three beats of bar 38 and on to bar 47) as continuing the pursuit for closure to the phrase begun in bar 30.

The strong cadence in bars 47–48 has an inescapable thetic quality signaling that an expected event — the event toward which the first theme as a whole and bars 30–38 in particular have been leading — has taken place. Yet this thetic quality is fleeting; in spite of the caesura (bar 48), the sense of anacrusis continues unabated.

What has been prepared has begun to happen, but evidently it will not take shape until further preparations are undergone. It turns out that 39–59 are more anacrustic to the second theme than they are thetic to the first theme. Calling bars 39–59 a bridge on the grounds that at bar 39 B-natural appears (and will persist), establishing a new tonic, and that their paired-phrases structure breaks down (to recommence at bar 60), one can sketch the relationship among bars 1–38, 39–59 and 60ff. as shown in Figure 17.

FIGURE 17

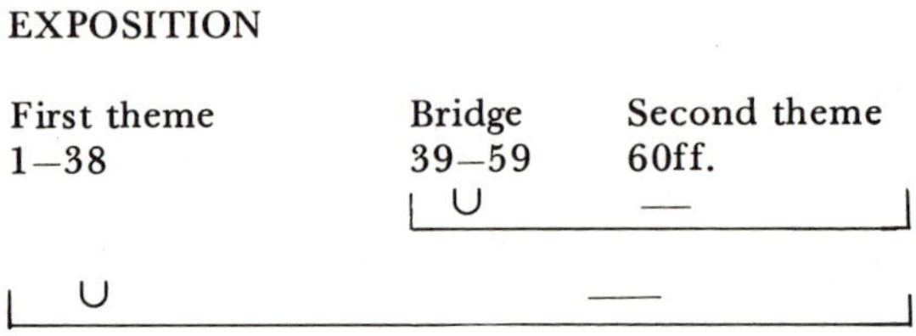

EXPOSITION

First theme	Bridge	Second theme
1–38	39–59	60ff.

The shape projected by the first theme, bridge and second theme has already occurred within the first theme. The first four-bar unit features a persistent six-four chord. Although the unstable chord does not resolve in bar 4, the themelike melodic and rhythmic shape of bars 1–4 makes them sufficiently analogous to a subphrase that the listener takes bars 5–8 to be its pair. Then when bar 9 begins as a repetition of bar 5, and out of it spins an extended subphrase answering bars 5–8, the listener realizes that bars 5–8 begin the event summoned by bars 1–4 but also prepare a soon-to-arrive event. The shape, sketched in Figure 18, is exactly like the shape projected by the first theme, bridge and second theme.

FIGURE 18

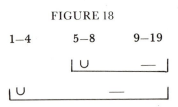

(ii) *The Movement as a Whole*

The same shape is projected by the exposition, development and recapitulation. By continuing the eighth-note motion at the end of the exposition (bar 97, Figure 19), and writing five transitional measures whose continuous notes flow directly into the development, Beethoven blurs the onset of the development as much as that of the second theme. Yet the tonic is unequivocally restored and the first theme, easily recognizable because of its chiseled rhythmic pattern, returns. These two aspects of bars 103–07 make the listener hear them at first as the usual, expected repeat of the exposition which is to form the

FIGURE 19
Beethoven, Quartet, Op. 59/1/i

usual pair with the first statement of the exposition. In other words, the beginning of the development sounds like the arrival of what our knowledge of the conventional practice leads us to expect.

But arriving on this familiar ground does not feel particularly comfortable because the ground itself, with its six-four harmony, unclear subphrasing and weak pairing, is not very comfortable. Consequently, the listener, expecting the entire exposition to be repeated, is both surprised to hear the putative exposition repeat veer into what can only be the development section at bars 107–8 and also relieved to hear the latently unstable first theme break down into patent instability. The sense of arrival changes quickly into a sense that further preparations are necessary before a firmer, more satisfying and less fleeting arrival can take shape. The development provides such preparation. It is unusually long. Only 4% of the other 1801–08 development sections are even a few bars longer than the exposition; Beethoven's is half again as long. It ends with an extraordinarily long retransition (bars 222–53; see Figure 20). Only 7% of the 1801–08 retransitions are longer than sixteen bars; Beethoven's is twice that length. During these thirty-two bars, the dominant harmony is prolonged and builds steadily mounting and eventually very intense pressure toward the tonic and the recapitulation.

Although the harmony (a six-four chord again) is unstable and although the first violin masks the onset of the recapitulation by repeating in its first bar the same figure it had in the last bar of the retransition, the onset of the recapitulation is clear, and it is clearly the arrival of what the development has prepared. Like the conventional recapitulation, its unclouded tonic harmony responds to the dominant harmony controlling the end of the development (bars 222–53). Like the conventional recapitulation, its well defined four-bar groupings are a return to a clearer, simpler organization after the structural vagueries of the development. And just as the recapitulation is the arrival of what the development has prepared, so the two together constitute the event prepared by the exposition's progression to and closure on the dominant. Except for the fact that the exposition is not repeated, these relationships (sketched in Figure 21) are closely analogous to those in most sonata-allegro movements composed in 1801–1808.

Beethoven's recapitulation differs from its analogues, however, in that, like the music it is reprising, it consists of a series of arrivals that consist of further preparation; that is, the arrival marks the beginning of what has been summoned by the immediate past, but it also prepares a coming event (see Figure 22). One might think that the sec-

FIGURE 20
Beethoven, Quartet, Op. 59/1/i

ond theme in the recapitulation would be less of an arrival than its exposition counterpart: in the reprise the second theme is in the same key (the tonic) as the first theme, and one might suppose that it therefore projects less of a sense of arriving at something new. In the standard sonata-allegro movement of the Classic period, the second theme reprise must be in the tonic to resolve the tension created in the exposition by presenting a main theme in some other key. Yet the tonic by this point may sound overused. These two constraints lead almost every composer of the period to do something to make the tonic sound fresh for the second theme reprise. Sometimes the first theme reprise is abbreviated or suppressed altogether; sometimes the first theme is recapitulated in a key other than the tonic; sometimes the

FIGURE 21

Exposition	Development	Recapitulation

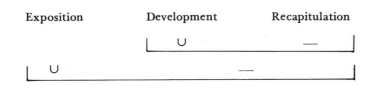

end of the first theme or the bridge emphasizes remote keys. In Op. 59/1/i, Beethoven solves this problem by moving so firmly into the lowered submediant (D-flat) within the first theme reprise that the return of the tonic prepared in the bridge and taking place in the second theme, sounds fresh and satisfying. Contrasting to the relaxation of tension in the D-flat passage,[2] the return to F is the image of a revitalized impulse. Here once again a prepared future begins to take shape. Joseph Kerman calls attention to the fact that D-flat is the main key of the development, and so when D-flat is resumed within the first theme reprise, the passage in F at the beginning of the recapitulation is reinterpreted to be the mediant of D-flat, and not the tonic.[3] By making the tonic at the second theme the first unequivocal tonic in the recapitulation, Beethoven enhances the sense of arrival it projects.

But the second theme in the recapitulation, unlike that in the exposition, turns out to be analogous to bars 5–8, to the bridges in the exposition and recapitulation and to the development: an arrival that turns into a preparation for a subsequent arrival. Just as the end of the exposition (bars 91–97) uses first theme material both to round out the exposition and to begin to build pressure toward the development, so the corresponding measures in the recapitulation (bars 338–47) build toward another point of arrival. The rising sequence and crescendo in these measures thrust forward so powerfully that the sense of preparation completely overpowers the sense of rounding out. A climax more powerful than that of the second theme is prepared, and it takes place beginning in bar 348, the onset of the coda. The shape of the recapitulation is sketched in Figure 22.

FIGURE 22

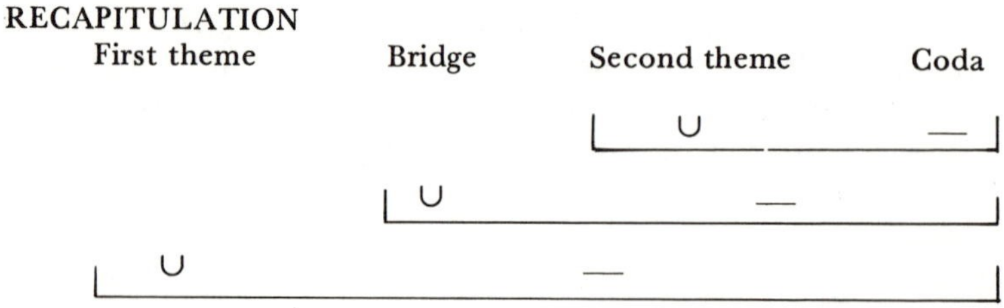

RECAPITULATION

| First theme | Bridge | Second theme | Coda |

The coda sounds like a final arrival — the future strained toward for so long is finally taking actual shape — because it states the movement's main theme harmonized, for the first time, by a root position tonic chord. Until the coda, the first theme has been ambiguous: its melodic and rhythmic contours and the phrase structure they imply have been unequivocally themelike, while the persistent six-four chords harmonizing it have made it relentlessly and, what is perhaps even more disturbing, uniformly unstable. A themelike quality generally involves a rhythm of alternating mobility and stability. Such a rhythm finally occurs in the first theme material in the coda, for the firmly stable statement of this material leads to an unstable six-four chord in bar 368, which in turn launches a cadenza (see Figure 23).

Six-four chords are conventionally used to begin cadenzas, particularly at the end of concerto movements but also elsewhere in Classical music. Beethoven's six-four chord and cadenza in bars 368ff. allude directly to this convention. Six-four chords since the very first bar of the movement turn out to have been implying precisely such an energy-releasing flourish as the one Beethoven gives us in bars 368–84. Thus, the coda deals with the first theme's ambiguity in two ways: it states the first theme melody in a stable harmonic context, and it satisfies the expectations generated by the six-four chord. Because it resolves this ambiguity, because it unleashes the energies whipped up during the development and recapitulation and because it has a clear and satisfying shape of its own, the coda is the concrete event that its past has called into being. That toward which the past has yearned, groped and struggled really happens.

(2) Future-orientation Coinciding with Past-orientation

A quick comparison of Figures 17, 18, 21 and 22 shows that the movement as a whole is made up of iambs nested with iambs:

Groups that successively comprehend more and more of the movement all consist of three parts:

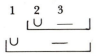

In each case, arrival happens, yet does not happen, at the beginning of the second of the three parts (i.e., bar 5 within the first phrase, the

FIGURE 23
Beethoven, Quartet, Op. 59/1/i

bridge within the exposition, the development within the movement as a whole and the second theme within the recapitulation). This ambiguity is similar to and yet the exact opposite of the ambiguity created in the Op. 1/2/i Trio movement: there an arrival at once does not happen (the new unit or section is heard initially as a continuation of the preceding one) and yet does happen (the prepared, yet fresh event actually takes place, one realizes in retrospect). In both the Trio and the Quartet the arrival of the prepared event is somewhat disguised, but the disguises are different: at the beginning of the exposition and recapitulation in the Trio one is not aware of beginning, but of having begun; in the Quartet one is clearly aware of beginning, but what begins is not fulfillment but a fresh push toward fulfillment. In the Trio the blurring intimates that what has already happened is continuing to happen — the past is in control — while in the Quartet the mask over the arrival suggests that what is to happen has not been sufficiently prepared — the future is in control.

In the Quartet, each successive instance of the complex relationship of preparation to arrival is more comprehensive in that it embraces more of the whole movement. Each successive instance confirms that the previous, less comprehensive one is indeed a salient aspect of the movement's process. Such confirmation is important because the very complexity of the nested iambs makes their effect unsettling. For example, because of the ambiguity generated by the first theme's uniform mobility, listeners cannot be confident they have grasped its shape. By nesting the first phrase's nested iamb into another iambic unit, and this one into another one, the movement transforms what is at first tenuous, unstable and unusual into a structure that is, in the context, firm, regular and normal. Just as the more comprehensive iambs clarify the less comprehensive ones by confirming their importance, so also the smaller ones confirm and clarify the larger ones. The iamb comprehending the whole movement would be shadowy and implausible had the smaller iambic units not begun to establish the viability of this shape. Without this confirmation, the arrivals at the recapitulation and coda would not serve as a metaphor for actualizing what their past has prepared. By making the implausible into the normative, the piece suggests that the movement from the past into the future it prepares is not so simple and straightforward as most of Beethoven's predecessors and contemporaries imagined and liked to suppose it was.

Taken together, the series of iambs nested within iambs project a temporal process that is as future-oriented as the front-heavy sections of the Op. 1/2/i Trio are past-oriented. To be sure, the second anacrusis in each complex of iambs is somewhat past-oriented: it is the beginning of an arrival; an arrival is by definition prepared by the past, and an event cannot be experienced as an arrival unless the person living it is in some sense past-oriented; one must experience its relation to what summoned it, or it does not feel like an arrival. At the same time, one must experience its separation from the past, or the event will not be an arrival but only a continuation of what has already been happening. And, in the case of Beethoven's second anacruses, the arrival is not only distinct from the past, but its texture and quality are even more controlled by what is coming than by what has happened. The very existence of the second anacrusis shows that the past has inadequately prepared the future; if further preparation were not necessary, there presumably would be no second anacrusis. The sense that further preparation is necessary bespeaks an orientation toward the future in light of which the past's preparations and the present's arrival are felt to be in some way deficient. In short, the orientation toward the future is so strong that the arrival of what ought to be fulfilling (that is, the beginning of the second part within each group) does not obviate the need for a further fulfillment. The second anacrusis suggests that more energy is required to summon the future than the first anacrusis spent or even envisioned. Before the new can happen, one must redo, and thereby intensify, the past's preparations (as bars 5–8 and 258–61 and the bridges do and as the second theme reprise does), and sometimes one must even cover the same ground again (as the opening theme is stated three times over a six-four chord before a stable, satisfying version of it, harmonized by a root-position chord, is attained).

But, in the end, the movement does not align itself with Schopenhauer's pessimistic judgment that the struggle to achieve a viable fulfillment is ceaseless. Although the movement toward the future is more convoluted and difficult than the late eighteenth century in general liked to imagine, an event that profoundly responds to the gropings of its past does take shape in the coda.

Like the second anacrusis in the various nests of iambs, the coda seems to be an image both of living from the past and of living toward the future. It is an image of living from the past in that it repeats and satisfies the past's struggles, and one must hear its relations to its past in order to hear it as the arrival of that which the past has summoned. It is an image of living toward the future in two ways. First, it is a transformed version of the very past that summons it into being; by repeating the first theme (though it also alters that to which it returns by replacing the six-four chord with a root-position chord), it reconvokes the future-orientation that characterizes the onset of the exposition, the development and the recapitulation. Second, the rising sequence of the coda's first ten bars (bars 348–57) and the dominant harmony extending from bar 357 to bar 368 generate a future-directed push that culminates in the cadenza of bars 368ff. But unlike the second anacruses, in which a future-orientation dominates a past-orientation, the coda maintains a balance between the two; here, living from the past and living toward the future are felt with equal force.

The effect of this coda on the movement as a whole is very different from the effect of the Op. 1/2/i coda. The earlier coda has a past-orientation in that it alludes to a first theme motif and resolves the tension created by the front-heaviness of prior sections. But this past-orientation is not very strong: the first theme motif is recalled rhythmically, but not melodically, and because the coda's first four bars do not respond to the preceding passage nearly so much as they push forward and because it is the coda as a whole that responds to the preceding front-heaviness, there is almost no sense of arrival in its first four bars. Having little sense of arrival implies that the relation to the past and its tensions is much looser at this point in the Trio than at the onset of the Op. 59/1/i coda. Past-orientation at the beginning of the Op. 1/2/i coda is subordinate to future-orientation. And the movement as a whole, once the coda has transformed its previous front-heaviness into end-heaviness, is far more future- than past-oriented. The front-heaviness turns out to be a temporary condition that is presented in order to be overcome, and the movement as a whole is more conspicuously end-heavy than its parts are front-heavy. By the end of the movement, one is experiencing the contrast between what is and what will be in the way a revolutionary experiences it.

While the Op. 1/2/i coda turns a past-orientation into a future-orientation, the coda in the Op. 59/1/i Quartet is a gesture in which a past-orientation and a future-orientation coincide: the onset of the latter coda is a thrilling moment precisely because it explicitly and immediately redoes its past in such a way that the past's instabilities are removed, and at the same time the future-orientation characterizing this past is sustained. A future-orientation and a past-orientation happen simultaneously; they equally characterize the same gesture; they balance one another; and their effects are completely congruent. The cleavage between the two orientations vanishes. Because of the coda, the movement exemplifies a temporal process in which the reasons motivating talk about revolution disappear because the distinction between revolutionary change and other change fades away.

One way to appreciate the significance of this image is to compare it to Martin Heidegger's analysis of temporality. In *Being and Time*, Heidegger contrasts the temporality of the authentic self to that of the inauthentic self.[4] Human existence is inauthentic, he says, when a person chooses to be in the way that "one is" and adopts as his own not only patterns of behavior but also a fundamental way of being that are dictated by the invisible yet powerful they-self (*"das Man"*).[5] Such a human existence is inauthentic (*"uneigentlich"*) because it does not comport with the fundamental, ultimately inescapable fact that existence is "my own" (*"eigen"*). The inauthentic self understands it-self in terms of the world, and so it understands its own behavior and motivations as examples of public events. When it looks ahead to what it will do and what will happen to it, the inauthentic self expects established patterns to perpetuate themselves and assumes that these patterns actualize human existence. This way of experiencing the temporal process is past-orientated: although the inauthentic self makes decisions and is not literally dominated by past events, it bases its decisions on an understanding of itself that comes from its relation to external processes, and acting out of this self-understanding means that the self experiences every event as a continuation of the past.[6] The self is not explicitly aware that it has decided to understand itself in terms of that which is not itself, yet, it, and not the "they" or the world, is responsible for this fundamental decision as well as for the particular decisions based on this basic self-understanding.[7] The self's responsibility for itself is not lessened by the fact that the inauthentic self cannot imagine any other way of being.

Authentic human existence, according to Heidegger, understands itself primarily in terms of itself. In this way of being, my outwardly visible acts, however routine and analogous to other events they may appear, are grounded in the decision to become myself, a person who is radically unique, regardless of any outward appearances to the contrary. The self I am becoming is that unsubstitutable self that is no more when I die. Heidegger emphasizes the phenomenon of anticipating one's death or being-towards-death not because he wants to dwell upon the futility of human existence but because this kind of radical future-orientation discloses the uniqueness (and freedom from the world) of that which becomes impossible upon dying.[8]

Although I may understand myself in this way, and not in terms of what I do in the outer world, nevertheless I still am always in the world so long as I am at all. Consequently, the basic decision to be simply myself always generates concrete decisions that are more future- than past-oriented, for being myself and being also in the world involves the search for the deed that will actualize the radically particular self I am and that must therefore be in some sense novel and unconventional.[9] Because inauthentic human existence cannot imagine deciding and acting on the basis of a profound grasp on one's self and one's uniqueness, it cannot see the respect in which the authentic self's deed is novel; to inauthentic human existence, every act is past-oriented. Even when it looks and plans ahead, the inauthentic self expects a future that is dominated (though not determined) by the past. The authentic self, even when it acts in the world and can therefore be interpreted as acting out the implications of the past, is future-oriented.

The disillusionment many revolutionaries experience is based on the inadequacy of even the most profound change to actualize the future-oriented self completely. To the extent that one's public manifestations can be compared to other public selves, they cannot successfully express one's unique self. Heidegger would interpret such disillusionment as a fall into the world, for it judges the becoming of the authentic self in terms that are inappropriate to it. Authentic human existence anticipates only itself and does not anticipate full concrete actualization; so it is tranquil and experiences no crisis when public events fail to objectify it. It knows that by its very nature a subject cannot become an object.

The effect of Beethoven's Quartet, Op. 59/1/i, differs from both the revolutionary's despair and Heidegger's tranquility by projecting a temporal process in which living toward the future and living from the past need not be at odds. While both Heidegger and the disillusioned revolutionary deny that concrete manifestations do or can coincide with the authentic self, the effect of the Quartet is to deny their denial. The movement's temporal process resembles one in which a past-orientation — an awareness of what I have been and what others have been in public view — is not, after all, irrelevant to my future-oriented decision to be myself. The one bears on the other. And, most important of all, what I do before the eyes of the past-oriented world is, or can be, what I am in my inner future-oriented process. Such an integration of external and internal processes is generally believed to be elusive. But Beethoven's movement at least makes it plausible.

Making this synthesis plausible cuts across the grain of the common-sense assumption that the full arrival of that which the past has prepared means the end of a future-orientation. Common sense says that if the goal of past striving takes complete concrete shape in public time, there is nothing left forward to which to look in private time. Beethoven gives us a temporal process in which a fulfillment is so complete that any need for further fulfillment is obviated, yet a future-orientation persists. It is a temporality in which one can look ahead and plan ahead and be oneself in relation to what one is becoming at the same time that one is completely content and at peace with the present. That common sense says such a temporality is nonsense does not mean that it is. The Quartet movement, Op. 59/l/i, may help us to accept it as a possibility.

Notes

1. Beethoven's procedure here resembles that in many of Haydn's sonatas, namely those in which the set of paired phrases in the dominant after the bridge uses the same motif as the first pair of phrases. With both composers, the harmonic contrast is a kind of departure in spite of the melodic similarities. But unlike Beethoven, Haydn usually introduces a motif in the exposition closing that is sufficiently different that it conveys a sense of arrival — but not of return, for the new key prevails.

2. See Rosen, *op. cit.*, pp. 79–80.

3. Joseph Kerman, *The Beethoven Quartets* (1971), p. 99.

4. Heidegger, *op. cit.*, pp. 67–68.

5. *Ibid.*, pp. 165–67.

6. *Ibid.*, pp. 386–87.

7. *Ibid.*, pp. 312–13.

8. *Ibid.*, pp. 294, 306–07, 311, 378–79.

9. *Ibid.*, pp. 84, 116–17, 158–59, 185.

CHAPTER II

Heroism Prevailing /
Heroism Falling Short

1. The "Archduke" Trio, Op. 97, First Movement

IN THE first movement of the "Archduke" Trio (1811), one climax stands high above the others — the one at the beginning of the recapitulation. Other climaxes along the way are weakened or suppressed. The passages leading up to the peak sustain the push toward a goal for an unusually long stretch. As fulfillment is postponed, the musical relations become more complex and less analogous to events in other pieces and seem to suggest that struggles and risks are required to achieve completion. The climax, when it comes, stands forth brilliantly and organizes the entire movement into a single, sweeping arch. The movement's temporal process is like one in which a deciding agent actualizes a future that expresses the agent fully and that responds to its past completely, but only by taking enormous risks and exerting extraordinary effort. Evidently, without such efforts, the self would be incompletely actualized and to that extent alienated from the concrete temporal events that occur.

The motif carrying both the struggle and the arrival of what is fought for has heroic connotations. This motif identifies itself with the hero in all of us, or at least elicits our admiration for the hero. The opening melody could be a soldiers' marching song or even an American football fight song. Such a banal text as, "On to victory; we will fight and win today," is not unthinkable for this tune, although the musical relations quickly become too tangled to support such doggerel. The grand sweeps up and down the keyboard in the bridge, bars 32–40, the thick arpeggios in bars 84–94 of the exposition closing

99

and the extended dominant washing through wide musical spaces in bars 162–76 of the retransition associate themselves with heroics. And the jubilation projected by the turgid texture, the swelling volume and rising register in bars 275–84 of the coda celebrate a victory only heroism could win. The movement as a whole, then, is an aural metaphor for a temporal process in which it is so difficult to create a future, as opposed to simply allowing forces analogous to natural causes to control the future, that only a heroic will can sustain the long struggle and in the end impose itself on a recalcitrant reality. Only a heroic will can give the outer world a shape congruent with its own. Revolution demands heroism.

The struggle which the movement projects comes to its end and makes its goal happen at the recapitulation (bar 191). The power of this climax results from the disturbing shape of the exposition and the extraordinarily long development section (it is a larger proportion of the whole movement than are 95% of the 1809–14 development sections) that the exposition generates.

The exposition is troubling because its arch has no peak. It can scarcely be called an arch, but the term suggests itself because the first theme and bridge thrust toward an arrival (an arrival to be surpassed by a subsequent one, to be sure) and the exposition closing (bars 60–94) has the relaxation, fluency and triumphant character that are appropriate for music that follows a climax. Yet there is no arrival. There is a dark hole in the center of the exposition.

It all begins with the pedal-point B-flat sustained by the off-beat eight-notes in the piano during the first eighteen measures. The melodic and rhythmic contours of the first four bars make them into a unit, particularly in an Allegro moderato tempo (see Figure 24). The conventions practiced by Beethoven's contemporaries would dictate that a subphrase end in bar 4. The persistent B-flats deny the listener a cadence in bar 4 (if those B-flats were changed to E-flats, the character of the entire movement would be changed). The pedal point makes what would have been a subphrase as mobile at its end as in its middle, and so one can speak only of a "*quasi*-subphrase." But, given the melodic and rhythmic contours and the expectations created by conventional practice, one must call it a subphrase of some sort.

Although the absence of a clear cadence in bar 4 is decisive in making bars 1–4 a quasi-subphrase rather than a conventional one, there are two other contributing factors. First, the opening four-bar unit is divided into two parts which balance each other but which are not symmetrical. The first part begins on the downbeat, while the second has an upbeat. The first part has seven beats, the second nine, and

FIGURE 24
Beethoven, Trio in B-flat for Violin, Cello and Piano, Op. 97, first movement

this asymmetry considerably increases the mobility persisting in bar 4 in spite of the whole note and the quasi-cadence. Second, bar 5 is a condensed version of bars 3–4, and bar 6 at first echoes and then alters bar 5. This procedure makes bars 5–8 less like a relatively closed group that responds to bars 1–4 as a group and more like a continuation spinning out of bars 3–4.

The first phrase (bars 1–8) ends on a dominant harmony that is prolonged for five measures before the phrase paired to it begins. Because of the return to the tonic and the opening tune, the sense of pairing is very strong at the onset of the second phrase. The concomitant sense of arrival dissipates, however, and the two phrases form a "quasi pair," analogous to the relation of bars 1–4 to bars 5–8, when the second phrase's last measure (bar 21) repeats the first phrase's ending on the dominant, instead of reaching closure on the tonic, and gives way to a twelve-bar extension. The onset of what becomes the bridge (bar 33) is dovetailed to tightly into this extension that the mighty descending arpeggios in bars 33–42 must be heard less as an arrival than as a continuation of the first theme's forward thrust. Moreover, the first theme's structure — with its quasi-, not conventional subphrases, its asymmetrical parts within quasi-subphrases and its extension — is almost as loose as the bridge's. There is no clear-cut alternation of paired and non-paired material (such as there is in many contemporaneous expositions; see Figure 16 for an example) that would make the first anacrustic to the second and the second thetic to the first.

The onset of the second theme is equally unclimactic. The bridge completes establishing G, the key of the second theme by bar 43 (see Figure 25). G is protracted for six measures, and then we are given almost three measures of "filler" music that rises melodically to close the gap between the D ending the bridge (bar 49) and the B beginning the second theme (end of bar 51). The filler measures anticipate the repeated note motif that the second theme features and arrive on B a beat before the second theme begins on the same note. In these two ways, the filler measures spoil somewhat the freshness of the second theme and lessen the sense of fulfillment it can project. Just as the pedal-point in bar 4 weakens the closure there, so these filler measures weaken the sense that preparation is ended and that the point of arrival is reached when the second theme begins.

Moreover, the character of the second theme is that of a jaunty little dance, hardly appropriate to a climax generated by the heroic struggles of the first theme and bridge. It sounds more like a temporary interruption of the movement's forward thrust, a postponement rather than a statement of its climax.

The second theme's tonal center confirms its non-climactic quality. In almost every 1809–14 sonata movement, a first theme in a major key is followed by a second theme in its dominant. Beethoven's is in the submediant. The root movement from I to VI is weak, and the sense that in going from the first to the second one has gotten anywhere is correspondingly weak.

Nevertheless, the exposition has some features that pair the first-theme-plus-bridge to the second-theme-plus-exposition-closing as well

FIGURE 25
Beethoven, Trio, Op. 97/i

as attenuations of these aspects. Beethoven suggests the pairing of the two parts of the exposition by making the second theme more stable than the first theme in several important respects. Its subphrases are as unambiguously paired as the first theme's are strangely paired. The parts of its subphrases are perfectly symmetrical. The subphrases begin with upbeats, none on downbeats, as do the first theme's phrases. The second theme has less rhythmic variety (like 65% of the 1809–14 second themes, compared to their first themes), less skipwise motion (like 58%), less sequential motion (like 54%), and more continuous motion (like 70%). All of these features contribute to the second theme's stability relative to the first theme. While, as the percentages indicate, it is not unusual for an 1809–14 second theme to have any one of these features, it is extraordinary for it to have so many stabilizing features.[1]

Given the stability of the second theme relative to the first theme, the two sections are heard as paired, just as bars 1–4 are, in some respects, paired to bars 5–8. But the elements attenuating this linkage make it a "quasi-pair", a larger-scale counterpart to the pair of quasi-subphrases in bars 1–8.

Up to this point, the movement has consisted again and again of a musical gesture summoning its pair into existence — the image of a past and a free agent conjuring up a future –– but the pair failing to materialize clearly. Yet there are enough hints of a pair partly emerging that listeners feel confirmed in having expected a pair. Both the sense that a pair is being working toward and the sense that it does not unequivocally appear with the second subphrase or the second phrase or at the beginning of the bridge or the second theme create a musical image of an increasingly intense struggle.

In bar 60 a reminiscence of the first theme (see Figure 26 and compare the cellos in bar 60 with bar 3) marks the onset of the exposition closing. Although the paired phrasing of the second theme ends with bar 59, the beginning of the exposition closing is dovetailed into the end of the second theme as firmly as the second quasi-subphrase is set into the first in the first theme and as the onset of the bridge is set into the end of the first theme, and so the exposition closing cannot be heard as a point of arrival. It behaves like a continuation spinning out of the second theme. Yet it has a distinctive character which sets it off from the second theme, just as the second quasi-subphrase and the bridge can and must be distinguished from the first quasi-subphrase and the first theme, respectively. With its broad melodic gestures (bars 60–67), its scales in thirds and in contrary motion (bars 67 and 76) and especially its thick arpeggios (bars 84–93), the mood it projects is that of celebrating a triumph. It does not sound like a climax, but rather like the jubilation that comes after a victorious climax. Like the exultation that leads from a peak to a calmer level of intensity, it would be an entirely appropriate gesture to follow a central point of arrival. In this respect, the exposition closing seems to live from its past — a past in which a climax has taken place.

But no such past has occurred! No victory has been won. The exposition closing is no more an unequivocal point of arrival than is the second theme. That toward which the exposition has been heroically struggling has not unambiguously taken place, and such heroics can be fulfilled only by a decisive victory.

Consequently, music whose character appropriately follows a climax and releases tension functions instead to increase confusion, frustration and excitement. For celebrating an unactualized victory creates a void within the exposition. It makes the non-happening of a goal more palpable than would have a straightforward continuation of the struggle toward a goal. At the end of the exposition the absence of fulfillment is more of a present force than is the hope for fulfillment in the future. Continuously led by the heroic connotations of the music to expect a fulfillment and certainly expecting no celebration until after the victory is won, the listener is bewildered. The canons of continuity to which the music itself appeals are violated.[2] Does the heroic, but thus far futile, struggle to actualize a future that is continuous with and responsive to its past suggest that fulfillment and continuity are not both possible — that fulfillment can come only if the future is apocalyptically severed from the past? Or does it suggest that fulfillment is only to be dreamed, not concretely actualized, but that the imagined fulfillment can be celebrated? Or that heroics are a sham — that the appeal to heroism is to be understood as ironic? Or that our ordinary understanding of both continuity and heroism must be rethought and refelt?

Superficially, the exposition resembles a tidy structure, but it is in fact a nearly chaotic struggle. The development section, lacking any paired phrases or even any internal cadences, appears to be even more disorderly. Yet it is organized to some extent by the tonal centers it emphasizes. First, it reviews B-flat, then G — the two main centers of the exposition — then emphasizes the dominant of B-flat during the lengthy retransition (bars 170–90). This extended dominant is justified by the absence of the dominant within the exposition at the ends of the quasi-subphrases in the first theme and even more by the absence of F from the second theme. The emphasis on the dominant in the retransition decisively reverses the trend toward increasing chaos experienced during the course of the exposition and develop-

FIGURE 26
Beethoven, Trio, Op. 97/i

ment. At the same time, its very length builds pressure toward a return of the tonic.

The return to the tonic in bar 191 is a point of arrival (see Figure 27). The shimmering shadows which, at the end of the retransition (bars 181–90), fall over the struggling, heroic arpeggios and scales (bars 156–80) vanish in the light of day; everything becomes clear, definite and positive. The event toward which the first 190 bars have been struggling begins unambiguously to take place in an actual and visible world. Launching the recapitulation, this point of arrival is carried by a tune that figuratively exemplifies heroism.

Because it is the first point of arrival that sounds unambiguously climactic at its onset and nothing happens to alter this character, it is tremendously forceful in spite of the fact that it is played softly. The climactic character would, of course, be attenuated if the exposition and its ambiguities were recapitulated literally, and the reprise differs in small but consequential respects from the exposition. These

changes make the difference between a section that projects fulfillment and one that projects struggle towards fulfillment. Because the
changes are small, clean strokes, the fulfillment is tightly connected to
the content of the preceding struggle: when the past's future arrives,
it is more profoundly related to the past than one living through the
struggle could imagine. In fact, the path to the goal is so long and tortured that only a visionary could imagine any future that would
genuinely respond to it, and only the most willful visionary could
imagine one achieved with such simple strokes.

The first of these changes is that the reprise of the first theme is em-
bellished with violin and cello parts. The cello adds the low E-flat at
the end of the first subphrase, so that there is no unstable six-four
chord here as there us in bar 4 of the exposition. As a result, bars 191–
94 are heard as a conventional subphrase, not a quasi-subphrase. The
eight notes that are added to decorate the melody in bar 193, stopping
abruptly in bar 194, enhance the mobility felt at the end of the sub-

phrase and hence its pairing to the consequent subphrases. The structure of the first theme is already more definite. Its shape is sharpened by the fact that the second phrase (bars 204–09) is not extended, as it is in the exposition, and the line between the end of the first theme and the beginning of the bridge (bar 210) is crisper. In these respects, change is more definite and continuity is more structured. Yet Beethoven has not lapsed into a continuity that is merely conventional: like its exposition counterpart, the second subphrase (bars 195–98) spins out of the F to G motion ending the first subphrase, and the bridge begins before the second phrase has finished a standard eight-measure course.

The second difference is the conventional difference between an exposition and its reprise: the second theme is recapitulated in the tonic. This change enables the listener to recognize that the two themes are much more closely related than it would have been possi-

FIGURE 27
Beethoven, Trio, Op. 97/i

ble to suspect during the exposition. For now one hears that the two themes span exactly the same notes — from D to the F below (compare bars 222–25, Figure 28, with bars 1–2 and 191–92 in Figures 24 and 27). In other words, the interval that is articulated by the first five notes of the first theme is restated in a prolonged form in the first four bars of the second theme. Consequently, the second theme is no longer a puzzling interruption of the first theme's struggle towards a goal, as it is in the exposition, but a varied renewal of the first theme's journey.

The closing (bars 230–67) continues this journey and celebrates the victory it is concretely establishing. Its jubilant mood, so confusing in the exposition, is now palpably appropriate.

The jubilation reaches its peak in the coda (bars 268 to the end), which begins with a forceful restatement of the main melody, its heroic connotations at their most explicit, and ends with an inverted

FIGURE 28
Beethoven, Trio, Op. 97/i

statement of the D to F interval (i.e., the F to D articulated by the piano right hand, bars 283–86). See Figure 29.

Heroism has had its way. Although struggles persist for two thirds of the movement, and although during its course the signs that they might end have been confusing rather than promising, the persevering hero has prevailed in the end. He has concretely established a form that is as firm as it is unprecedented. Violating accepted canons of continuity and so trembling on the brink of chaos that again and again during the movement it appears that the future will be apocalyptically severed from its past, he creates in the end a new kind of continuity. In the new continuity, things do not lead where they seem to. Greater perseverance and strength is required to establish the past's future than the past leads one to expect. Premature arrivals are exposed to be unearned climaxes that are not in fact climaxes at all, and their very untimeliness exposes the terrible void created in the present when the past's future is unexpectedly and indefinitely postponed.

The movement as a whole projects a temporal process in which courageous decisions are made in full awareness of the context created by the past, and these decisions summon a future that does justice to both the deciding self and the past but that is very different from a future in which routine, everyday expectations are fulfilled in a conventional way. It is a temporal process in which revolution is possible and in which change can be profound without apocalyptically denying continuity.

2. The "Hammerklavier" Sonata, Op. 106, First Movement

The heroic connotations of the four-measure fanfare (Figure 30) opening the Op. 106 Sonata in B-flat (the so-called "Hammerklavier," 1818) are at least as explicit as those of the "Archduke" Trio's first

FIGURE 29
Beethoven, Trio, Op. 97/i

theme. The mood of the fanfare is hopeful, perhaps even naively optimistic. But the overall effect of the movement is disheartening and depressing, for its most resounding climax comes too early. This premature and hence false point of arrival happens at the beginning of the recapitulation where the fanfare returns in full dress in the tonic. But it comes in the wrong harmonic context — it comes too soon in the harmonic structure. It sounds willful, and not genuinely responsive to its past. This mistimed climax is soon followed by another climactic statement of the heroic fanfare, but this one is in the wrong key (B minor) and seems for this reason to reinforce the disheartening effect of the first climax. The tonic returns soon after the B minor fanfare, but no sense of arrival marks this moment. The movement's only unequivocal arrival comes too late; it occurs within the coda, after the movement's energies have entered an irreversible decline. The timing costs the fulfillment its sense of satisfaction; it is too late to be celebrated or enjoyed.

FIGURE 30
Beethoven, Sonata in B-flat for Piano, Op. 106, first movement

It is depressing for heroism to make its goal happen only to have temporality rob it of its significance. The sadness is deepened by the ironic fact that the heroic fanfare itself plays a decisive role in generating and marking the very structure that ultimately saps heroism of its positive effect. This aspect of the movement — the climactic statements of the heroic fanfare are out of phase with the very structure that the fanfare generates — is crucial to the temporal process that the movement projects. In order to develop the concepts that are needed to characterize this temporal process, the following paragraphs will describe the articulating caesuras and harmonic pattern that structure the movement, the way the fanfare launches and demarcates this structure and the three climactic fanfares that are so disturbingly ill-timed vis-à-vis this structure.

The movement's harmonic structure is derived from the fanfare in the following way. The opening fanfare consists of two members of a rising sequence, the second a third higher than the first. Each member ends with a falling third. The harmonic structure of the exposition and development consists of falling thirds — from B-flat (first theme) to G (bridge, second theme and exposition closing) to E-flat (bars 128–90 of the development) to B (bars 201–26 of the development).

The sections controlled by G and E-flat are set off from their preceding sections by conspicuous caesuras (bars 38 and 135). The only prominent articulations before the reprise, these caesuras are marked by forceful statements of the heroic fanfare. The major passage (bars 201–26) is set off from its preceding section by a *rallentando* and a change in texture, and it too contains a restatement of the fanfare (bars 213–26 — the retransition). These articulations and fanfares put the structure of falling thirds into a high relief. The precipitous turn to B-flat for the recapitulation and return of the fanfare (bar 227) sounds willful and unconvincing because it makes no sense in terms of this succession of falling thirds. Entering without a tonicizing preparation, the sudden B-flat seems to ignore the entire harmonic succession articulated by the prior sections of the movement.

Had the reprise of the heroic fanfare in B-flat been harmonically prepared, it would have been triumphantly climactic. The untimeliness of this climax is quickly confirmed, as the recapitulation of the first theme soon slips into G-flat (= F-sharp), which comes to function as the dominant of B. The fanfare returns in B minor at the beginning of the bridge (bar 267), making the twelve bars of B-flat at the onset of the recpitulation sound like a temporary interruption within a passage controlled by B.

To say that there are major articulations only when the fanfare recurs is to imply that the bridge, second theme and exposition closing constitute a single musical gesture, as indeed they do. The bridge, after blaring the fanfare in B-flat, turns abruptly to the dominant of G (bars 37–38). It does not modulate to G, and G is established as a tonal center only by the sheer dint of repetition. To avoid monotony, Beethoven casts the reiterated motifs tonicizing G into paired phrases (Figure 31, bars 47–63). If G were established as a tonic before these paired phrases began, they would be analogous to the second theme in other movements. But instead they serve to tonicize G, in order that the pair of subphrases in bars 63–66 and 67ff. may function as a second theme. Both because there are paired phrases within the bridge and because the first two beats of the second theme (beat 4 of bar 62 and beat 1 of 63) overlap the last two beats of the bridge, one does not hear bar 63 as the clear beginning of a new section. The onset of the exposition closing overlaps the end of the second theme just as tightly, for, without a caesura of any kind, the closing spins out of an extension of the second theme's second subphrase.

Making the bridge, second theme and exposition closing into a single gesture would make a passage grotesquely out of proportion with the passage to which it is paired were it not that the first theme (Figure 32, bars 5–17), together with its closing (bars 18–34), is unusually long relative to the second theme and exposition closing. In other words, the first theme is so long that if the bridge were grouped with it, this section would be out of proportion to the second theme plus exposition closing. It is the opening fanfare that propels and justifies the long first theme, which then justifies the length of the first theme closing, which in turn justifies grouping the bridge with the second theme and exposition closing. The opening fanfare motivates the long first theme and its closing in the following way: it ends not on a cadence (or it would be a subphrase paired to bars 5ff.) but on an unstable six-four chord. Although the fanfare is harmonically static and generates no harmonic propulsiveness, the two members of its sequence begin on D and F, suggesting a melodic line whose goal is B-flat. The first theme begins on this B-flat.

The first subphrase (bars 5–8) is rhythmically relaxed, and its melodic range is narrow, so much so, in fact, that by itself it could not generate the long expansion that extends its pair (bars 9–17). This expansion (last three beats of bar 12 to the downbeat of bar 17) can only be heard as the product of the fanfare's melodic directedness and inconclusive six-four chord. That the fanfare serves this function can be confirmed by imagining that there were no fanfare and that bars 5–17 were the opening of the movement and noticing how unsatisfactory such a beginning would be.

The expansion of the second subphrase consists of a number of repetitions, and these generate enough energy to propel the uncommonly long first theme closing, which in turn is needed in order that the first theme plus closing be long enough to warrant the amalgamation of the bridge, second theme and exposition closing. In other words, the way the fanfare propels the lengthy expansion of the second subphrase is analogous to the way this expansion propels the still longer first theme closing, and to the way this closing's length propels the even longer section that begins with the bridge and comprises the rest of the exposition.

The lengthy expansion of the second subphrase would have obliterated the paired-subphrases structure if Beethoven had not projected this structure so clearly and conventionally: the most conventional means (harmonic instability) is used to endow the first subphrase's ending with the mobility that makes it form a pair with the second; the second subphrase begins with the same melody that starts the first

FIGURE 31
Beethoven, Sonata, Op. 106/i

one, as do its counterparts in two-thirds of the 1815–23 movements;[3] like 85% of the other first subphrases and like 80% of the other second subphrases, Beethoven's divide themselves into two parts which balance each other (even though the second part of Beethoven's second subphrase is extended by five downbeats); and both parts have upbeats of the same length, like two-thirds of the 1815–23 first themes. (In this last respect, Beethoven is so conventional that he is in fact unconventional! For while the usual procedure is to give the two parts of a subphrase upbeats of the same length, it is also the usual procedure — that is, it is the practice followed in 69% of the 1815–23 expositions — to have at least one subphrase in either the

FIGURE 32
Beethoven, Sonata, Op. 106/i

first theme or the second theme in which the upbeat to one of its parts is longer than the upbeat to its other part.) In short, Beethoven expands the second subphrase, but, in order not to weaken the pairing of the two subphrases, he does not, as others do, relieve the symmetry and rigidity of the second subphrase in any way other than the expansion.

Unlike most first theme closings, Beethoven's does not release the tension developed by the preceding material. On the contrary, it continues to build tension until bar 31 when, without reaching a climax, the rate of increase of energy begins to decline. Suddenly, the fanfare strikes up again. An energy-producing and not an energy-absorbing gesture, it is not a point of arrival. Rather, it marks a new beginning.

Nor is there a point of arrival at the beginning of the development, for there the allusion in E-flat to the fanfare (bars 134ff.) also marks a new beginning, not a climax. Although there is no climax within the development, the rate of building tension rises and falls, so the sense of struggling toward a goal is not without some rhythmic shape. But it is primarily the emerging coherence provided by the falling-thirds structure that promises that the struggle will have an end and its goal will happen.

The effort to establish this goal at the beginning of the recapitulation is heroic. The effect of making this attempt before the context defined by the harmonic pattern is ready for it is devastating. In bar 227 (Figure 33), the hero sounds like a bully. Failing to be adequately responsive to what has (and has not yet) happened, he exposes himself as unperceptive or at least insensitive.

The return through the G-flat of the first theme recapitulation to B, at the onset of the recapitulation bridge (bar 267), deepens the effect of the premature climax. The *fortissimo* fanfare in bars 267–68 (Figure 34) is a sort of negative climax, the most intense moment of dramatizing the abortive positive climax.

FIGURE 33
Beethoven, Sonata, Op. 106/i

In bar 270, the succession of root movements by falling thirds recommences: B gives way to G. But this G, it turns out, functions not only as the submediant of B but also as the dominant to the supertonic of B-flat. In bars 272–73, G progresses to a C minor chord, and the harmonic structure of falling thirds gives way to root movement by falling fifths (though the bass moves by falling thirds). The C (II of B-flat) progresses to F, the dominant of B-flat (bars 274–82), and thence to B-flat in bar 283. Unlike the B-flat at the beginning of the reprise, this B-flat is earned. The progression beginning in bar 270 establishes B-flat as a tonic, and this progression is fitted into the succession of falling thirds in such a way that the progression by fifths is heard as the continuation of the movement's basic harmonic structure.

Thus B-flat emerges as the final goal of the movement's underlying harmonic progression. The future that has been expected and struggled for comes to pass beginning in bar 283, but because the music slips into the paired phrases of the bridge, then into the second theme reprise and the recapitulation closing without ever suggesting a climax, the goal is not actualized as a separate, distinctive event. The listener has been led to expect a climactic point of arrival both by the powerful energies that gather as the movement runs its course and by its analogies to contemporary movements in which fulfillment is embodied in a distinctive, identifiable event. This expectation is disappointed again: the first putative climax (the fanfare beginning the reprise) has come in the wrong harmonic context, the second (the B minor fanfare) has consummated the tension without relaxing it, and now the return to the tonic is accomplished without a climactic point of arrival.[4]

By bar 352 the movement has run its course. The harmonic struc-

FIGURE 34
Beethoven, Sonata, Op. 106/i

ture is complete. The energies are spent. The reprise of the first theme is longer than its exposition counterpart, so the recapitulation by bar 352 is longer than the exposition, and the unusually long development and the recapitulation are together weighty enough to balance the exposition plus its repeat.

Yet the music goes on. A fifty-bar coda makes a last, desperate attempt to state a climax congruent with the heroism of the movement's struggle. The coda has four sections and reviews, in reverse order, the materials used in the various non-theme passages of the movement: first, the cadential motif ending both the exposition and the recapitulation is extended (bars 352–61); then the motif associated with the exposition and recapitulation closings is recalled (compare bars 362–72 with 100–11 and 332–43); then, the bridge motif (bars 373–76) and finally the opening fanfare (bars 377–405) assert themselves. The onset of each of these motifs breaks the flow carrying the previous one. Nothing in any section justifies the next one. This succession of motifs would be disturbingly incoherent were it not that each one reminds the listener of an earlier passage and that the succession repeats, though it also reverses, a pattern already established by the movement.

The coda is, then, an inverted and compressed version of the movement. If one remembers the original order in which these motifs appeared, one would expect the fanfare to be the end of the succession, and in this sense the coda can be said to "lead to" the heroic flourish. The final statement of the fanfare is, to that extent, a point of arrival. Unlike the arrival of the fanfare at the onset of the recapitulation, it occurs in a harmonic context that supports and does not contradict its climactic quality.

But this climax is disappointing. For while the succession of motifs in the coda "leads to" the arrival, there is no forward thrust in the coda pushing toward this point. On the contrary, the prior parts of the coda dissipate the movement's energies. They do not build pressure toward a climax. Instead, their character is that of leading away from a climax.

Yet the only positive, nearly triumphant climax that has taken place is one that is out of phase with other aspects of the movement and in that sense is not sufficiently responsive to its past. To be "led away" from such a climax is to feel disillusioned. Such a feeling might involve either a resigned hopelessness or a persevering determination to try again. Given the heroic connotations of the movement, one hears the disillusionment as a willingness to struggle on.

Perseverance with no illusion of success is especially vivid when, near the end of the coda, the heroic fanfare makes its final appearance (bars 386–89). The restatement of the fanfare in bar 377 is interrupted by a rising sequence built out of a fragment of the fanfare (Figure 35). Each member of the sequence is two bars long. The first two members (bars 378–79 and 380–81) consist of a loud and a soft statement on the same pitch. This pattern ends in bar 383 when the soft echo is displaced by a measure of silence, followed by the next member of the sequence and another silent bar. The suddenly loud interruption of the fanfare in bars 378, the mounting intensity of a rising sequence and the instability created by the silent bars push into the reprise of the full fanfare (bar 386). Bars 378–85 sound like a determined but desperate effort to set up a final point of arrival, a genuinely climactic return.

But when the fanfare returns (bar 386), it is anything but climactic. Its first two beats are replaced by a murmuring figure; the first statement of the very rhythm (♪ | ♩·) that makes it sound like a fanfare is suppressed. When the right hand does state this rhythm, it therefore sounds like a continuation of the fanfare that is started and interrupted in bar 377 and is now being restored and completed. It is as though bars 378–85 had not happened; their efforts to set up a climax turn out to have been futile. Moreover, the last two chords of each fanfare stated in bars 386ff. are immediately repeated, but the restatements (unlike those within the sequence of bars 377–85) are loud, while what they restate are soft. This reversal of the loud-soft pattern underscores the non-fulfilling quality of the fanfare's arrival. To hear the difference between loud-soft and soft-loud groups is to hear mounting excitement juxtaposed to angry disappointment. The unnaturally loud "echo" is the sound of trying to force a resolution, of trying by brute force to yank a concrete fulfillment out of the temporal flux. But it is also the sound of a determination that knows it is failing. Instead of calmly resigning itself to futility, the determination grimly continues to assert itself and becomes the sound of a desperation that — unlike most desperations — is cool, measured and not at all frantic.

The desperation is fitting in spite of the fact that heroics have established a point of arrival, for the arrival feels too late. The heroics turn out not to have been in control, even though Beethoven has created here, as in the "Archduke" Trio and elsewhere, an image of the temporal process in which the decisions of a moral agent make occurrences eventful, and what happens is the result of human decisions, not of fate or nature. The temporal process exemplified in the "Hammerklavier is not one in which publicly manifest occurrences articulate an atemporal pattern that is more important than

FIGURE 35
Beethoven, Sonata, Op. 106/i

events in the public arena. The temporality of the "Hammerklavier" does not resemble a process in which publicly manifest occurrences are assumed never to be more than the distorted reflection of a reality that is fundamentally interior and in principle unactualizable in the outer world.

But although what happens would not have happened had the hero not perseveringly struggled, what happens is not the satisfying fulfillment toward which he aspired. For in the temporal process of the "Hammerklavier," unlike that of the "Archduke," decisions evidently have effects which the hero does not and perhaps cannot foresee: the heroic fanfare generates a harmonic structure that turns out to be at odds with the fanfare itself and consequently deprives the fanfare's return in the tonic of its triumphant character. The way the fanfare propels a long first theme which in turn justifies the amalgamation of the bridge, the second theme and the closing and the way the fanfare generates the harmonic pattern of falling thirds suggest a process in which a hero sets into motion forces that have a life and power of their own and that ironically undercut the hero's power to assert his will effectively. We do not know why: Is it because society is inherently recalcitrant, or because other heroes are making contradictory, hence neutralizing, decisions, or because of some aspect of the intrinsic nature of temporality? In any case, the actual outcome does not bring with it a sense of fulfillment. What happens is not celebrated. Evidently, the temporal process projected by Op. 106/i is one in which it is not always possible for the actual change wrought by a revolution to correspond exactly with the revolutionary's vision.

Yet the sonata's hero heroically continues to care about what happens. His response to his failure is, if anything, even more courageous than his struggle. He does not retreat from recalcitrant temporality to atemporal interiority, nor comfort himself with the notion that it is the struggle, not the goal, that counts, nor content himself with partial fulfillments, nor resign himself to supposedly inevitable distortions of his goals. The reason for his failure to endow the future with his own shape is not that he struggles less valiantly or less perseveringly than the Archduke's hero, and so he cannot see his failure as evidence of weakness or a temporary lapse. Having thus denied himself every way of softening the effect of non-fulfillment, his ultimate posture is profoundly uncomfortable. The temporal process projected by the "Hammerklavier" demands heroism that is in fact more profound than anything intimated in the more optimistic — some would say more idealistic — temporality of the "Archduke."

Notes

1. Rosen, *op. cit.*, p. 70, says that whatever contemporary practice may have been, Haydn, Mozart and Beethoven usually write second subjects that are more intense than their first subjects. He cites the *Apassionata* second subject as an example that is both more lyrical and more intense than the first subject. The "Archduke" second subject is not really an exception to his generalization: while in the respects listed it is more stable than the first subject, the rhythm of the second theme's melody and its harmony are both somewhat more nervous than the broader, grander first theme. In the music of Beethoven's contemporaries, the second theme is also stabler in some respects and less stable in other respects than the first theme, and the particular set of stabilizing or mobilizing features varies from one sonata to the next. On balance, the second theme is generally stable relative to its first theme, though in some cases the two sets of paired phrases are equally stable (and equally mobile).

2. The strange way the exposition closing seems to respond to an event that has not taken place (as well as the ambiguities associated with the second theme) makes one uncomfortable with Kerman's judgment (*The Beethoven Quartets*, p. 94) that the "Archduke" is as normal as the Quartet, Op. 59/1/i, is radical and that the Trio is less dynamic and disruptive than the Quartet.

3. In earlier first themes, even more second subphrases begin with the same melody as the subphrases to which they are paired. In 1795–1800, 80% of the movements have at least one pair of subphrases melodically linked in this way; in 1801–08, 71%; and in 1809–14, 86%.

4. Rosen hears the B minor fanfare as the movement's climax. For him the movement's coherence is achieved by the B-flat/B-natural clash that results from the falling thirds structure from B-flat through G and E-flat to B and is echoed in other ways (the B-natural of the exposition's second theme in G clashes with the first theme's B-flat; the sudden B-flat at the end of the exposition clashes with the B-natural of the long section in G; the B-natural of the second ending to the exposition contrasts to the B-flat in its first ending; the exposition closing juxtaposes B-flat and B-natural in bars 104 and 110; the first theme closing is "already contaminated by the B major which still lies in the future" [*op. cit.*, p. 418]; and the clash is sustained for the ten bars of the C-flat/B-flat trill in the coda, bars 362–71). The B minor fanfare is the movement's climax in the sense that its explosion realizes the magnetic force of the still unresolved tension of the B-natural (p. 414). Although the B-flat/B-natural tension is most intense at this point and although the rest of the movement, he says, is firmly in the tonic, the clash persists to the end. Rosen aptly describes the sonority of the coda as "dissonant but without pathos" (p. 420).

Rosen does not emphasize the conventional procedures that Beethoven uses in virtually every section of the movement, and consequently for him the movement's analogies to other movements form no part of the experience he is analyzing. The listener who is reminded by Beethoven's use of contemporary conventions of other sonata-allegro movements is also reminded of the arrivals that constitute the foci of these movements; for such a listener the fact that the expectation for fulfillment is persistently disappointed in the "Hammerklavier" is as important as is the B-flat/B-natural clash, whose persistence is the particular way that fulfillment is avoided while coherence is nevertheless achieved.

CHAPTER III

Creating Several Futures at Once:
Disparate Shapes Confirming One Another / Disparate Shapes Contradicting One Another

---

1. Piano Sonata in E Minor, Op. 90, First Movement

THE FIRST movement of the "Archduke" Trio, with its profound sense of struggle, its premature celebration and its other discontinuities, projects a temporal process that is far more complex, convoluted and, in the end, satisfying than the temporality envisioned by any of Beethoven's musical contemporaries. The temporal process of the "Hammerklavier" Sonata's opening movement is even more complex, as it projects a temporal process in which the movement from past to future is profoundly affected by the decisions of a free agent, yet the future does not fully bear the shape of the hero who aspired to actualize himself through its events, and yet again the doer does not retreat from the partly frustrating, partly fulfilling temporal process to an atemporal inner world.

The temporal process of the first movement in the Op. 90 Piano Sonata (1814) is even more complex. It interweaves two shapes. Each shape is unambiguously projected by conspicuous and patently significant gestures, and some of the musical events that generate the one make little sense in the other. As the music progresses, the future consists of articulating and completing each shape, and as two disparate shapes emerge, the process seems to consist of moving from a past to two different futures. The process is persistently complex in the sense that the two shapes do not yield a single, overarching form that embraces both of them, nor is one of them subordinated to the other. Yet

125

the two processes are not mutually irrelevant: some musical events are operative in both of them. It turns out that the temporal process is not fundamentally irrational: while the two futures maintain their independence and each is as fundamental and real as the other, they do not contradict each other. Instead, there are elements of each that clarifies the other's shape and supports its viability. To a certain extent, then, the disparate shapes are integrated.

(1) The Sonata-Allegro Shape

One shape is a conventional sonata-allegro form (see Figure 36). The movement contains many cliches common to all the sonata-allegro movements published in Vienna between 1809 and 1814. Both themes identify themselves as themes by pairing four-bar subphrases to each other. In several instances, the second subphrase begins with the same melody as the subphrase to which it is paired (in Figure 37, compare bar 1 to 5, 17 to 21 and, in Figure 38, 55 to 61), and by 1814 this way of marking paired groups was very conventional indeed. Like a standard bridge, bars 25–54 offer a melodic transition between the two themes by anticipating the second theme (bars 25–28 are an inverted form of bars 55–58) whiled horizontalizing the tonic chord ending the first theme. The bridge begins in the key of the first theme and establishes the key of the second theme. There is a written-in accelerando in the bridge (bars 29, 30, 33, 34, 37, 38), and to the extent that this surge releases the energy confined within the rigid channels of the first theme's paired phrases structure, the bridge forms a group with the first theme. The section closing the exposition helps to pull the exposition together into a unit by responding to both themes: it alludes to the first themes's material (compare bars 8–12 to 69–70, 73–74, 75–78), and, because of its slower melodic and harmonic rhythm and less nervous texture, it relaxes the level of intensity sustained during the second theme.

Three B minor chords dearly and decisively mark the end of the exposition (bars 79–81, Figure 39). No false cadence followed by transitional material obscures this articulation.

Like half of the development sections in sonata-allegro movements published in Vienna between 1809 and 1814, the Op. 90/i development begins with an introductory gesture (bars 82–84), and, like all of them, it ends with a retransition. That this retransition does not sustain a dominant pedal makes it somewhat unusual, but no means unique.

FIGURE 36

Sketch of Beethoven, Sonata in E Minor for Piano, Op. 90, first movement

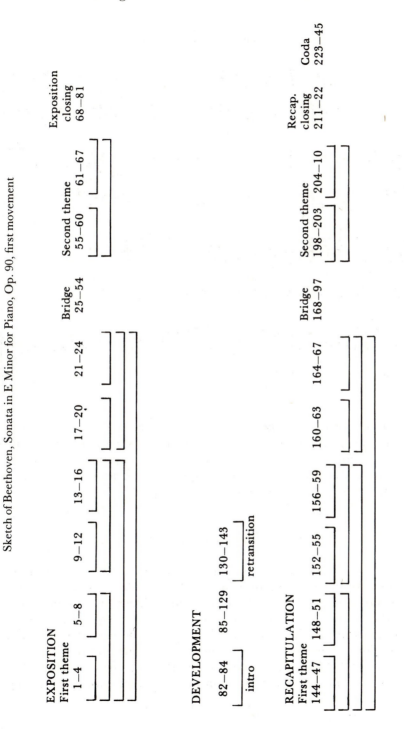

FIGURE 37
Beethoven, Sonata, Op. 90/i

The recapitulation comes at the end of a crescendo and a metrically ambiguous passage, so, like three-fourths of its contemporaries, it begins as a point of arrival. Both themes are recapitulated in the tonic without any abbreviation. The recapitulation bridge and closing correspond closely to their exposition counterparts.

(2) The Middle-heavy Tripartite Shape

Against the background of conventional procedures, four unusual events take place. In many respects the first theme sounds more like a second theme and the second theme more like a first theme. The second theme is in the "wrong" key–B minor instead of the G major that is standard for second themes following a first theme in E minor. The exposition is not repeated. And the articulations that mark the beginning of the bridge, the second theme, the exposition closing, the development and the recapitulation are all either unusually strong or

FIGURE 38
Beethoven, Sonata, Op. 90/i

FIGURE 39
Beethoven, Sonata, Op. 90/i

unusually weak. These unusual features do not make sense in terms of the sonata-allegro process that other features are propelling, but they are too conspicuous to ignore. On a first hearing, the presence of some features that generate a sonata form along with other features that gainsay one may make the movement seem incoherent. If one segregates, at least temporarily, the features that do not fit into the sonata form from those that do, and sees how the former interact with each other, then one hears a form consisting of three clearly defined sections. The first section (bars 1–24) consists of the first theme. The second section is six times as long, and goes from the beginning of the bridge to the end of the first theme in the recapitulation (bars 25–167). The third section runs from the recapitulation bridge to the end of the movement.

The following paragraphs will amplify the four unusual features in the movement and show how in supporting one another they generate the second shape that superimposes itself upon the conventional sonata-allegro shape.

(i) The Two Themes

In the sonata-allegro movements published in Vienna by Beethoven's contemporaries, the second theme is almost always more stable in some respects than the first theme, just as a second phrase in a pair ends more stably than the first. Beethoven's practice in Opp. 1/2/i, 59/1/i, 97/i and 106/i conforms to theirs. Moreover, the second part of the exposition (second theme plus exposition closing) is always stabler than the first part (first theme plus bridge). Of course, the first theme or the first part of the exposition from one sonata may be more mobile than the second theme or the second part of the exposition from another sonata; the mobility of the one and the stability of the other is always relative to the other theme or part in the same movement.

The listener probably needs to be aware of the ways in which Beethoven's contemporaries made the second–theme–plus–closing more stable than the first–theme–plus–bridge in the same sonata in order to appreciate the fact that Beethoven reverses this practice and to feel how remarkable this reversal is. In his contemporaries' music, the greater stability of the second theme or of the exposition's second part is a function of a number of actors, not all of which need to be present in any one sonata. It may be longer (it is in 72% of the 1809–14 expositions). It usually begins and ends in the same key, while the first part begins in the tonic and ends in the dominant. Second theme subphrases usually begin with longer upbeats than the first theme subphrases in the same movement, and fewer second theme subphrases start on the downbeat. The second theme paired phrases usually (77%) have a closing that rounds them off and makes then sound finished before the exposition closing begins (only 44% of the first theme paired phrases have a few bars of closing material before the bridge begins), and the second theme closing is usually (87%) longer than the first theme closing. The second theme usually has fewer subphrases whose parts are unbalanced and asymmetrical (in the sense that one part has a longer upbeat than the other part). The motion in the second theme is usually more predictable and continuous; second themes usually have less rhythmic variety and less skipwise motion. The second theme usually has more instances of a second subphrase expanded beyond the length of the subphrase to which it is paired. Although some expansions are gestures in which forces gather for a push forward, generally they stabilize the pair in the sense that they make it end-heavy, and by loosening the rigidity of the paired-phrases structure they weaken the sense of pushing against the confines of a highly organized shape and thus reduce the pressure toward a more flowing musical gesture.

In many respects, the first theme of Beethoven's Op. 90/i is stabler than his second theme: it is longer (the first theme is twenty-four bars long; the second ends abruptly in its thirteenth bar); it has less rhythmic variety, less skipwise motion, fewer subphrases beginning on downbeats and more beginning on upbeats. There are no asymmetrical subphrases in the first theme to make it more mobile (only 27% of the 1809–14 first themes have, like Beethoven's, no asymmetrical subphrases) nor any expanded subphrases in the second to make it more stable (all but 30% of the 1809–14 second themes have at least one expanded subphrase). At the same time, there are other respects in which the first theme is more mobile than the second: it is front-heavy (the *ritard* in bar 15 and the fermata in bar 16 make bars 1–16 form a group paired to the group in bars 17–24; were it not for the *ritard* and *fermata* one might be able to hear 9–24 as a group paired to 1–8; as the first phrase stands, it is twice as long as the second (see Figure 37; none of the 1809–14 first studied are so front-heavy); its motion (like that in 70% of the other first themes) is less continuous, less predictable and more nervous than the flow in the second theme; and the abrupt changes of dynamic level in the first subphrase (bars 1–8) decrease stability (such changes are always noticeable and effective, yet their power to increase mobility is utilized in only 2% of the 1809–14 movements).

Taking all these factors into account, one must conclude that, contrary to contemporary practice, the factors stabilizing the first theme relative to the second outweigh those stabilizing the second theme. The greater stability of the first is especially obvious if one compares the degree of finality associated with the cadences ending the two themes. The second theme cadential figure (Figure 38; bars 66–67) is premature: it comes where one would expect a second pair of subphrases to begin. And while it is prepared harmonically by the dominant preparation in bar 66, the change of texture at bar 67 seems abrupt. The first theme ends with much greater finality, generated by a full cadential formula that is underlined by a *ritard* (bars 22–24). Such a degree of completeness is ordinarily reserved for the last cadence in a movement. In fact, the last eight bars of this movement repeat bars 17–24 literally.

The sense of completion in bar 24 is so strong that the continuation of the movement would seem willful and arbitrary were it not for the proportions of the first theme. Because the first phrase is sixteen bars long, one expects the second to be at least as long. But after only eight measures, the second phrase ends, and the bridge begins. The disproportionate brevity of the second phrase provides a strong link between the first theme as a whole and the bridge, for in an important sense the beginning of the bridge is the continuation and completion of the first theme. The strong continuity created by this linking contradicts the strong caesura created by the finality of the cadence in bar 24 and the rest with a fermata thereafter. In other words, the strong continuity on the section-to-section level overcomes the total absence of continuity on the note-to-note level at the end of the first theme.

(ii) The Key of the Second Theme

The situation is reversed at the beginning of the second theme: the note-to-note continuity is stronger, but the section-to-section continuity is weaker than at the beginning of the bridge. The bridge is comparatively long (relative to the whole exposition it is longer than 95% of the 1809–14 bridges; relative to the first theme, it is longer than 67% of the others) mostly because it goes on for ten measures after arriving at B, the key of the second theme. While these ten measures strengthen the tonicity of the second theme tonic, they also dissipate some of the energies generated by the modulation of bars 25–45, thereby weakening the thrust from the bridge as a whole to the second theme. Nevertheless, there is some sense of section-to-section continuity because of the powerful dominants in bars 51–54. The note-to-note continuity is stronger and more obvious; it is the result of beginning the second theme melody on the last note of the bridge's melody and of maintaining eighth-note motion across the articulation between the end of the bridge and the onset of the second theme.

In spite of the fact that this second theme in many respects is more mobile than the first, it is tonally stable. It is firmly in B minor. Its harmonic stability is a relief from the harmonic ferment in the bridge. It is also a contrast to the harmonic ambiguity characterizing the first theme. The movement opens with an E-minor triad, but the very next chord contradicts E: instead of the dominant of E, it is the dominant of G, and the first theme is solidly in G for almost two-thirds of its life.

The first theme having preempted G (the usual key for the second theme in an E–minor movement) and having avoided the dominant for sixteen measures, it is fitting that the second theme is in B, the dominant.

The second theme fulfills the function of emphasizing the dominant, a function usually performed within the first theme in a minor-mode piece, and the first theme exhibits within itself the relation of a minor key to its mediant, a relationship usually projected by the two themes together in a minor-mode piece. In the conventional minor-mode movement, the relationship of a first theme in minor to a second theme in its relative major invariably weakens the tonicity of the tonic, for the two themes are built on the same set of pitches (although they use a different center), and the music always tends to slide into the higher center, the major-mode tonic, for it is the stabler of the two. In one way or another, all minor-key movements must compensate for this weakening of the tonic. Beethoven's way is to expose the problem

baldly within the first theme and then to deal with it by using the tonality of the second theme to strengthen the tonic.

And strengthen it the second theme does. It is only half as long as
the first theme because it does not flirt with a second tonal center. It
is steadily, relentlessly, clearly and firmly in B. It ends quickly, and
does not expand itself by touching on other keys. Like only 18% of the
1809–14 second themes, it consists of only one pair of subphrases
(77% of the 1809–14 second themes consist of a pair of phrases, each
consisting of a pair of subphrases). It also ends abruptly; like only
23% of the 1809–14 second themes there is no second theme closing.
The exposition closing begins on the heels of the second subphrase.

(iii) No Repeat of the Exposition

The exposition ends in bar 80. Although the ending is clearly marked,
the forward thrust at that point is unusually great. Three features of
the exposition are particularly responsible for the forward movement
felt at its end, and together they account for the absence of an exposition repeat. First, the exposition is extraordinarily front-heavy: the
second theme is shorter relative to the first theme than 98% of its contemporaries; the exposition closing is shorter relative to the bridge
than 95% of its contemporaries; the second-theme-plus-exposition-
closing is shorter relative to the first-theme-plus-bridge than 95% of
its contemporaries. This lopsidedness presses the music onward.
Beethoven begins the development with a repetition of the last three
bars of the exposition (compare bars 82–84 with 79–82, Figure 39).
Although about a quarter of the development sections in Mozart's
piano sonatas begin with an allusion to the end of the exposition, only
12% of the 1809–14 movements use this technique. While easing into
the development is somewhat unusual by 1814, it serves well in Op.
90/i: it moderates the effect of the exposition's front-heaviness, for it
minimizes the sense that the exposition is over and that a separate
and distinct gesture has begun.

The second and perhaps more significant feature generating the
forward thrust felt at the end of the exposition is the force of the dominant on which the second theme has insisted. To go from this dominant suddenly into G major, which repeating the exposition would
entail, would generate serious discontinuity. Dealing with it would
have resulted in a piece very different from the one we have.

Third, the exposition ends with much stronger forward thrust than
the first theme. Given the comparative stability of the first theme and
the sense of finality conveyed by its cadence, the movement would

stop at the close of the first theme if an exposition repeat were in-itiated. The first time through the exposition, Beethoven overcomes the risk of sounding as if a second piece were beginning at bar 24 only because of the surprising brevity of the first theme's second phrase; during a repeat of the exposition, listeners would be less surprised by the first theme's front-heaviness, and familiarity would weaken the forward push generated by front-heaviness. Continuing beyond bar 24 the second time through would seem unmotivated and unwar-ranted.

(iv) The Articulations of the Movement's Sections

In the sonata-allegro movements written by Beethoven's contem-poraries, the end of the first theme, the end of the bridge, the end of the exposition, the end of the development, the various sections of the recapitulation and the beginning of the coda are marked in various ways. In any given movement, some of these points are more notice-able than others. It is not at all unusual, for example, for the end of the first theme and the beginning of the bridge to be more masked than marked.

What is unusual about the articulations in Beethoven's Op. 90/i is that all of them are unusually strong or unusually weak. A gulf separates the bridge from the first theme, the latter ending with a full cadence, *ritard* and rest with a *fermata*, and the bridge beginning with fresh melodic material (although with no change of harmony); the bridge is linked to the first theme neither by note-to-note continuity nor by thematic similarity. All the subsequent articulations until the recapitulation of the bridge are very weakly articulated. The caesura between the bridge and the second theme is disguised: no rest divides the two passages, and the last note in the bridge's top voice is identi-cal to the first note in the second theme's melody (bars 54–55, Figure 38). The end of the second theme paired phrased overlaps the begin-ning of the exposition closing (bar 67). The development begins by echoing the end of the exposition, maximizing note-to-note continuity at this point. There are no cadences within the development, and the retransition begins (bar 130) with no articulation and with no change of motif. The recapitulation begins (bar 144 in Figure 40) without a change of the harmonic root: twelve bars before the recapitulation, the tonic is regained and never left. Moreover, the retransition and the recapitulation use the same motif, so neither a change of melodic material nor a harmonic progression marks the beginning of the re-capitulation. Because the retransition has an unsettling rhythmic pattern which gives way to the movement's normal triple meter and because a crescendo in the retransition climaxes at the some moment, the reprise is a point of arrival. Nevertheless, the note-to-note continuity is so strong that the point is very weakly articulated.

Like their counterparts in the exposition, the beginning of the recapitulation bridge is strongly marked, while the beginning of the second theme and recapitulation closing are barely noticeable. The coda spins out of the recapitulation closing with maximal note-to-note continuity.[1]

FIGURE 40
Beethoven, Sonata, Op. 90/i

There are, therefore, only two major articulations: at the end of the first theme in the exposition and at the corresponding place in the recapitulation. These articulations divide the movement into three parts. Each part ends with the same eight-bar phrase; it is a gesture that signals completeness.

Within this tripartite shape, it is unproblematic for the second theme to have features usually associated with the first theme and vice versa. The second theme is the beginning of the long middle part of the movement, which the first theme reprise ends. The relative mobility of the one and the relative stability of the other are appropriate to their places at the beginning and the end of this middle section, respectively.

(3) Two Shapes Interacting

At the end of the movement, the listener has experienced two processes. In one, the future generated by the exposition and development
happens climactically at the beginning of the recapitulation and occupies the whole of the reprise. Irrelevant to this process are the facts
that the standard relationship between the relative mobility of the
first theme and the relative stability of the second is reversed, that the
first theme wobbles between E minor and G major while the second
theme is in the non-standard key of the dominant, that the exposition
is not repeated, that the strongest articulations occur between the first
theme and the bridge in the exposition and the recapitulation (not, as
is usually the case, at the beginning of the development and the beginning of the reprise) and that a gesture signaling completion closes the
first theme in both the exposition and the reprise, as well as the whole
movement.

In the other process, the future that happens at the beginning of the
recapitulation is generated by the second theme, exposition closing
and development, and it ends at the close of the first theme reprise.
Such a future is not weighty enough to balance the past to which it is
related, and the center of gravity in the group that begins with the second theme is not in the recapitulation, but in the development—the
group's middle section. Indeed, the process projected by the movement as a whole consists of one middle-heavy group nested into
another: the movement as a whole consists of three sections, of which
the middle one is the longest. This middle section consists of three
parts—the second-theme-plus-exposition-closing, the development
and the first theme reprise—in which the middle again overbalances
the other two, and the middle part of the middle section is middle-
heavy, for the introductory gesture opening the development (bars
82–84) is very short (53% of the 1809–14 development sections open
with a gesture that has an introductory character; 91% of these
analogues to bars 82–84 of Op. 90/i occupy a larger proportion of the
development as a whole), and the retransition (like all standard retransitions) is much shorter than the main part of the development.
See Figure 41.

Thus, on each architectonic level, the listener hears groups that
have three parts: a short anacrustic section, a long thetic section and
a short closing section that rounds out the group:

1   2   3

⌐∪ — ∪⌐

FIGURE 41

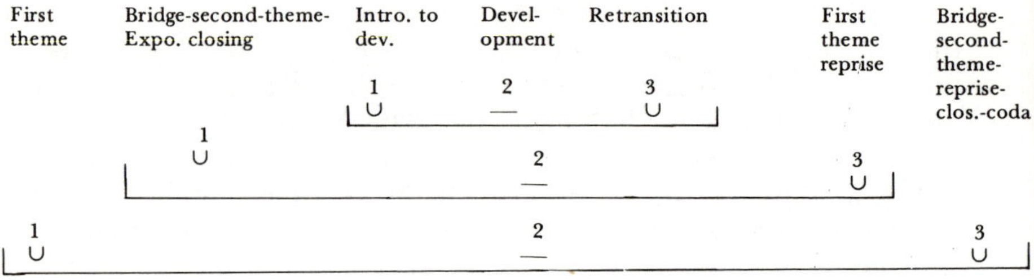

First theme	Bridge-second-theme-Expo. closing	Intro. to dev.	Devel-opment	Retransition	First theme reprise	Bridge-second-theme-reprise-clos.-coda
		1	2	3		
		⌣	—	⌣		
	1					
	⌣					
			2		3	
			—		⌣	
1			2			3
⌣			—			⌣

Each group consists of a past (the anacrustic section) that works toward a future, the realization of that future (the long middle section) and a second future (the third part) that rounds out the first future, realizing its implications without arriving at anything new or suggesting a fresh event. Because the middle-heaviness of these groups is so pronounced, the first part of each one, it turns out, is dominated by the future to which it leads, no matter how strongly or weakly it summons that future, and the third part turns out to be just as markedly past-oriented. On the three highest architectonic levels, the first part leads into an experience (namely, the second and third parts as a unit) which becomes past-oriented before it is over:

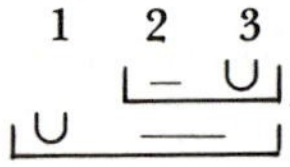

And the third part harks back to a past (the first and second parts as a unit) that was future-oriented while it was taking place:

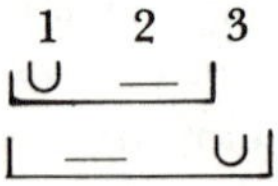

```
1   2   3
⌣   —  ⌞
⌞   —   ⌣
```

For example, on the highest level, the first theme is future-oriented, but the future to which it is directed does not finish actualizing itself until the end of the movement, and when this future is complete, it consists of a past-oriented experience (that is, the reprise of the second theme plus recapitulation closing plus coda look back to and are dominated by the exposition's second theme plus its closing plus the development and first theme reprise). At the same time, the past back to which the final part of the movement (that is, from the second theme reprise to the end) looks is part of a future-directed and end-heavy process (that is, the section beginning with the second theme and ending with the first theme reprise is a fresh event responding to and also overbalancing the first theme). While Op. 1/2/i transforms a past-orientation into a future-orientation, Op. 90/i insists on both orientations and allows neither to become subordinate to the other. While Op. 59/1/i leads into the coincidence of the two orientations, Op. 90/i superimposes each on the other and maintains the distinction between them.

The clues that one is hearing a sonata-allegro movement are as irrelevant to the middle-heavy tripartite shape as the features making the latter happen are irrelevant to the sonata-allegro shape. Neither pattern is more fundamental than the other. Yet the two also reinforce and support one another. First, the very fact that they are interwoven and are equally basic helps to make it plausible that the members of another interwoven and apparently incompatible duality — namely the past- and future-orientations that the middle-heavy shape projects — may also be as primordial as one another. Second, the sonata-allegro shape of Op. 90/i, like the middle-heavy shape, involves an interplay of past- and future-orientations.

The sonata shape leads the listener into a past-oriented experience in which what has happened is weightier than what is now happening and the texture of the present is controlled by the past in several ways: its first theme is beginning-heavy, and the exposition as a whole is beginning-heavy (the first theme is a larger proportion of the whole exposition than it is in 86% of the 1809–14 expositions; the first-theme-plus-bridge is longer relative to the second-theme-plus-exposition-closing than it is in 95% of the 1809–14 movements). In spite of the fact that the Op. 90/i second theme consists of two phrases of equal length, it is comparatively beginning-heavy, for in two-thirds of the 1809–14 second themes, the first phrase is shorter than the second. The ratio of the exposition to the recapitulation (excluding the coda) is greater here than it is in 57% of the 1809–14 movements, and the ratio of the development to the recapitulation (excluding the coda) is greater here than in 77% of the others.

The sonata shape of Op. 90/i also leads the listener into the experience of living toward the future, for there are other groupings that are as unusually end-heavy as the ones listed above are beginning-heavy. In spite of the strong caesura at the end of the first theme and the weak one at the end of the bridge, the first theme is paired to the bridge, and so it is relevant to the movement's process that the first theme is shorter relative to the bridge than it is in 67% of the 1809–14 movements. Similarly, the second theme is shorter relative to the exposition closing than it is in 68% of the 1809–14 movements. The development as a whole is longer relative to the introductory gesture that opens it than are 91% of the 1809–14 developments having an introductory gesture. The retransition occupies a greater proportion of the whole section between exposition and reprise than in 67% of the 1809–14 movements. The development is longer relative to the exposition than in 76% of the other movements, and the development plus recapitulation (including the coda) is a larger proportion of the whole movement than in 98% of the others. The recapitulation plus coda is longer relative to the exposition than in 93% of the 1809–14 movements.

The sonata-allegro process of the movement is, in short, characterized by both beginning-heavy gestures and end-heavy gestures. The two kinds of gestures are interwoven in such a way that neither outweighs the other. This superimposition of opposing kinds of groupings confirms the audial relevance of the way the various nested middle-heavy groups within the tripartite shape (see Figure 41) also combine and interweave beginning-heavy and end-heavy groups. The groupings and proportions of the sonata-allegro's exposition (see Figure 42) parallel and reinforce the way each level of the tripartite shape consists of a beginning-heavy group whose beginning consists of an end-heavy group:

```
1   2   3
|U  —  |
|  —  U|
```

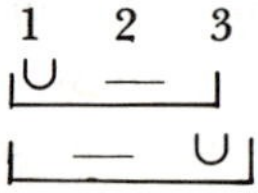

And the groupings and proportions of the sonata-allegro's development and reprise (see Figure 43) parallel and reinforce the way each level of the tripartite shape consists of an end-heavy group whose end-directed first part leads into a gesture that is beginning-heavy before it is over:

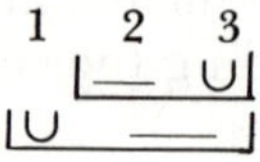

```
1   2   3
|—  U|
|U  —  |
```

FIGURE 42

```
First theme              Bridge              Second theme   —   Closing
|  U                            |
|         ———                                        U        |
```

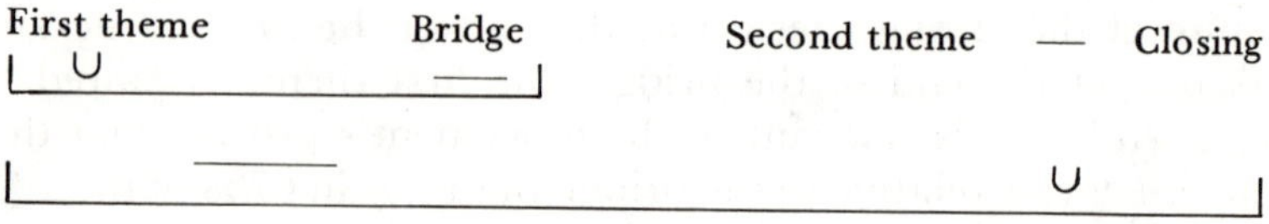

FIGURE 43

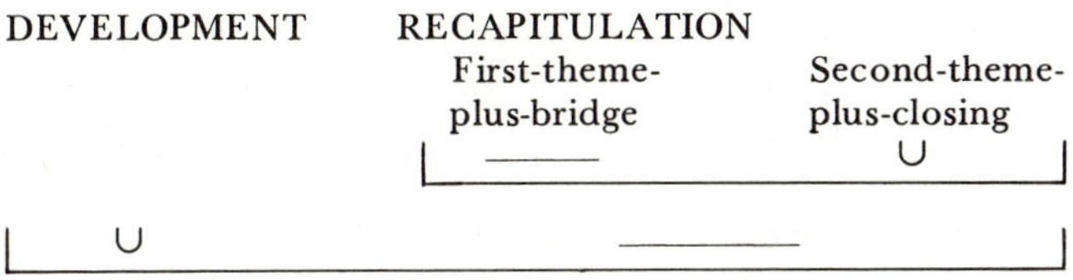

DEVELOPMENT   RECAPITULATION
First-theme-   Second-theme-
plus-bridge   plus-closing

The temporal process projected by the movement is complex in two ways. First, it has two over-all shapes and insists on them equally, so its beginning has two ways of completing itself — two futures. And, second, each movement to completion involves both a future — and a past-orientation. It makes two distinct features equiprimordial, and it makes living toward the future distinct from and equiprimordial with living from the past. Each of the two complexities makes the other more plausible. Because there are two complexities, the listener is more willing to accept each one and less apt to seek a resolution for either of them. The equiprimordiality of the two futures helps dissuade listeners from seeking clues that would determine whether it is a past-orientation or a future-orientation that is more basic. And the equiprimordiality of living from the past and living toward the future helps dissuade them from seeking clues that would determine which future is basic and which is subordinate.

In such a temporal process, one can not think of the future simply as that which an agent creates in response to his past, for the sense in which the future fully actualizes the agent and completes the past is seriously attenuated by the fact that a different future is simultaneously being created. Both futures are somewhat fulfilling and somewhat responsive, but the very fact that there are two of them means that neither is final. There can therefore be no celebration of a hero's struggle and victory, and Beethoven's movement closes with a somewhat perfunctory gesture that has come to signal completion without connoting consummation.

The movement is open-ended at its close in the sense that the two completions it has achieved do not obviate the need for new and further completions. To a certain extent, what the listener feels at the close of the movement is controlled by what has not happened. Yet the feeling at the end is controlled just as much by what *has* happened: concrete and satisfying completions have, after all, taken place. The temporal process is evidently unending and perpetually future-oriented, for the equiprimordiality of the two shapes prevents the movement from projecting even the possibility of a consummation that would ring the temporal process to a close. Yet the temporal process does not thereby become a ceaseless, futile struggle, for the completions actualized in it are rich and meaningful. Hearing an event as a completion entails an orientation to the past it completes, and this past-orientation is by no means displaced by the ongoing orientation toward the future.

This temporal process is one in which the concept of revolution is viable only if revolution means actualizing a change that is genuine and profound, but does not imply a change that is all embracing and final. For in this temporality no one completion takes up into itself all the salient tendencies of the past. Into the process in which a revolutionary change happens are interwoven other changes which are more or less profound and more or less irrelevant to the revolutionary change. The temporal deployment of human experience is evidently so intricate that any revolution is but one among several components of temporal actuality. No single change so comprehensively responds to all aspects of the past that further change is unthinkable. Revolution cannot end with its agents so living from the past that no further change is expected or worked toward. Revolution, in the image of temporality projected by Beethoven's Op. 90/i, begins and ends with both a past- and a future-orientation.

Common sense would tell us that if the concrete quality of present experience is controlled both by what has happened and by what has not happened, the effect of each must be attenuated by the other. Yet Beethoven's two shapes lead the listener into a temporality in which each is fully operative and neither weakens the effect of the other. Although the two shapes are persistently disparate, they work together to project a coherent — and extraordinary — image of the temporal process.

2. *String Quartet in A Minor, Op. 132, First Movement*

The A Minor Quartet, which Beethoven wrote in 1825, baffled his contemporaries. A number of the first movement's features seemed to contradict one another. It was hard to know which of them related themselves to each other, because many of the relations had never been heard before. Since then, listeners have become familiar with it, but the movement is still difficult to understand. Even when the contradictions are sorted out and the relationships clarified, complexities persist. The movement's temporal process turns out not to exemplify one in which revolution is possible and heroism effective, though it is such that one is not thereby excused from trying to bring about change nor acting courageously.

The movement's contradictions and the persistent difficulties they cause come into sharpest focus when one sees that this movement, like the opening movement of the Op. 90 Sonata, simultaneously creates two shapes. As the music unfolds, two futures come into expectation, and both come to pass. Both shapes consist of three sections — the same three sections, for the principal articulations in both structures, unlike the articulations in Op. 90/i, occur at the same points (end of bars 74 and 192). One is an end-directed and goal-oriented shape in which tensions generated by internal inconsistencies within the exposition are partially resolved in the second section (the development plus what will be called the first recapitulation; see Figure 44) and finally discharged in the third section (the second recapitulation plus the coda). The shape can be sketched as:

⌊∪ ∪ —— ⌋

Although the movement connotes anguish and pathos and not heroism, this process resembles that of the "Archduke" Trio's first movement in that it risks serious discontinuities as it struggles toward and finally achieves a fulfillment that is congruent with the struggling agent and his past.

Along with this linear, dynamic structure and in a counterpoint with its purposive march forward is a perfectly symmetrical structure whose center of gravity is the middle section. Two outside sections precisely balance one another and support the towering central section. Like the end-directed shape, this middle-focused one gets its impetus from a difficulty experienced in the exposition. This discrepancy, however, is resolved only in the second section, and the third section rounds out the movement without furthering the resolution. The first and second sections thus form an end-directed group that overlaps with a beginning-oriented group consisting of the second and third sections. This shape can be sketched as:

⌊∪⌊ —— ⌋ ∪ ⌋.

This middle-focused shape has the same double insistence on past- and future-orientations that characterizes one of the two shapes projected by Op. 09/i.

Unlike the two shapes in the Op. 90 movement, the two processes in this quartet movement do not reinforce one another. At the end the listener is called upon simply to recognize and accept their fundamen-

FIGURE 44

Sketch of Beethoven, String Quartet, Op. 132, first movement

EXPOSITION

Intro	First theme						
		2+2				1+2	
1—10	11—12	13—16	17—21		22—23	24—26	27—31
	intro	phrase a	extn.		intro	phrase b	extn.

| a | b |

tonal
center: a   a

DEVELOPMENT

Bridge	Second theme		Expo.clos.			
		2+6				
	2+2	2+8	7+5			
32—48	49—52	53—62	63—74	75—79	80—102	103—18
	a	b		intro		retrans.

a → d → F   F   F

FIRST RECAPITULATION

Intro	First theme						
		2+2				1+2	
119—120	121—122	123—126	127—32		133—34	135—37	138—
	intro	phr. a	extn.		intro	phr. b	extn.

| a | b |

e   e

Bridge	Second theme		Recap. clos.	
		2+10		
	2+2	2+12		
—159	160—63	164—77	178—88	189—192
	a	b		trans.

e → a → C   C   C

SECOND RECAPITULATION

Intro	First theme				Bridge	Second theme		Coda
		2+2	2+2					
193—94	195—98	199—202	203—06	207—14	215—23	224—27	228—32	233—6
	intro	phr. a	phr. b	extn.		a	b	

| a | b |

a   a   a   A   a

tal incompatibility and the irrationality of living simultaneously two contradictory temporal processes. The movement excepts itself from the generalization that Beethoven's sonata-allegro movements resemble those by Haydn and Mozart in suggesting the process wherein a deciding agent effectively shapes a coherent future that is responsive both to itself and to the past. A future that comprehensively actualizes the self and the past simply does not take place.

(1) The End-directed Shape

Several significant aspects of the quartet's exposition contradict each other and make it difficult to hear how its parts are related to each other: the first part of the exposition (first-theme-plus-bridge) seems to be generating a future, and the material in the second part (the second-theme-plus-exposition-closing) is stabler, as if it were actualizing that future; at the same time the first part is much longer and more climactic than the second, and the latter, though stabler, offers no point of arrival. Related to this difficulty is the unconventional key scheme: the bridge has themelike material in the subdominant, and the second theme is cast in the submediant instead of the mediant.

There are two recapitulations, and they progressively resolve these anomalies and the tensions they cause. The first recapitulation eases them, and the second removes them altogether. Stating, reducing and eliminating these anomalies constitute the goal-directed shape.

(i) The Equivocal Relationship between the Two Parts of the Exposition

In many respects the first theme is, as convention would have it to be, mobile relative to the second theme, and the second theme is stable relative to the first. The first theme is more mobile than the second in that it has more rhythmic variety, more skipwise motion, more sequential motion and more subphrases in which the upbeat to the first part (two downbeats) of the subphrase is either longer or shorter than the upbeat to the second part of the same subphrase. The second theme is more stable than the first in that its motion is more continuous and fluent (owing both to the fact that it has less rhythmic variety and to the fact that the caesuras between and within subphrases are weaker than in the first theme). The second theme has a lyrical quality (Kerman associates its accompaniment with a "slack Italian aria"[2]) that makes it unsuitable as a first theme but that is entirely appropriate in the second part of the expositon. The second theme is built of motivic elements used in the first theme. In fact, the second theme sounds like a less nervous, more relaxed redoing of the first theme. Thus, the contrast between the moods of the two themes does not generate tension, but instead represents the transformation of an energy-creating into an energy-dissipating event.

The relative mobility of the first theme and the relative stability of the second theme make the first part of the exposition form a pair with the second part, analogous to the way a phrase whose ending is mobile (compared to that of the next phrase) forms a pair with the more stable second phrase. In light of these features the exposition as a whole is a stable, end-accented pair of parts. This stability is supported by the way the second theme reworks the first theme's motif. It is also supported by the exposition closing, for it blends material from the first theme (compare bars 67 and 69 witrh 19 and 29, and 68, 70–72 with 1–8) with the material that rounds out the second theme (bars 57–62). Moreover, the second part of the exposition (that is, the second theme plus exposition closing) is an end-heavy group (indeed, the exposition closing is a larger proportion of this group than it is in 90% of the 1824–26 movements). This proportion enhances the stability of this part of the exposition, which in turn enhances the pairing of a relatively mobile first part (slow introduction, first theme and bridge) to a relatively stable second part.

There are, however, other respects in which the exposition as a whole is wobbly. Its first part is almost twice as long as the second; in only 7% of the 1824–26 expositions is the first part so large a proportion of the whole exposition. Such a drastically beginning-heavy group is anything .but firm footed. Moreover, the harmonic background in the first part consists of a complete progression that makes it a stable, end-directed section. This progression uses only root movements of a third: the harmonic roots move down a third from A (the controlling harmony in bars 1–29) to F (bars 30–37), then down another third to D (bars 40–43). The end of the bridge turns to the dominant of F, and thus creates the sense that one is moving up a third and returning to F and that the moment when the return is complete will be somewhat climactic. If Beethoven cashed in this expectation by beginning his second theme as a point of arrival, the pairing of the two parts of the exposition would have been strong and unmistakable. But he does not. The forward flow of the movement stops abruptly before the second theme begins (see Figure 45). The second theme sounds more like an interruption than a climax because of the sudden drop from *forte* to *piano*, because of the unresolved voice leadings in the upper parts of bar 47, because of the dawdling accompaniment figure in bar 48 and because of the comparatively gentle, static character of the second theme's tune. Beethoven somewhat cynically given us a second theme that denies the meaningfulness, perhaps even the existence of the first theme and bridge. The climaxes that occur in the first part of the exposition (bars 40 and 47–48) are stronger than anything that happens in the second part.

FIGURE 45
Beethoven, Quartet, Op. 132/i

(ii)   The Key Scheme

The ambiguity and insecurity projected by the equivocal relationship between the two parts of the exposition is intensified by an unconventional key scheme: the second theme is in F (the submediant) instead of C (the mediant, which is the conventional key for the second theme in minor-mode pieces), and the bridge dwells on the subdominant (d) for four measures (bars 40–43).

The standard progression from a minor-mode first theme to a second theme in the relative major generally supports the sense that the first theme is mobile relative to the second theme. Again, this effect is based on the fact that one of the forms of the scale of which the minor-mode theme is built consists of exactly the same pitches as those in the scale of which the second theme is built. Consequently, the dominant of the second key is a chord that makes perfectly good sense in the first key, and using this dominant thus creates little sense of modulation. The center of the set of pitches being used changes, but no new pitches are introduced. In other words, a minor-mode theme can slip almost imperceptively into its relative major mode (and as a result, many minor-mode sonata movements have either very short bridges, and go almost directly from a theme built on a minor scale to one built on the relative major, or very long bridges that move far enough away from the minor-mode tonic to make a crisp contrast to the relative major). Of the two centers, the second is by far the more stable. In fact, when the second center is articulated it is often so strong that it makes the first one seem to have been a temporary center. Had Beethoven used the standard key for his second theme, the equivocation concerning the two theme's relationships would have been eased in favor of the second theme's comparative stability.

To follow a theme built on A with a theme built on F is a somewhat more thorough change than following an A-centered theme with a C-centered theme would have been. Consequently, the tonal contrast between the beginning and the end of the exposition is somewhat greater in Beethoven's than in the standard procedure, and the thrust forward into the rest of the movement generated by that contrast is also a little stronger.

When the second theme is in the first theme's mediant or dominant, the second theme prolongs one of the pitches in the first theme's tonic and thereby strengthens the movement's tonic. Putting the second theme in the submediant deprives the tonic of this emphasis. Beethoven makes a problem of this deprivation by emphasizing D in the bridge, with the result that the three pitches prolonged by the exposition are D, F and A. In that this articulation of the D minor triad puts an emphasis on D that undermines the tonicity of A, which is explicitly stated in the slow introduction, it is a significant aspect of the exposition's wobble.

The three measures in D minor within the bridge also confuse the listener in another way. Dwelling on the subdominant always slackens musical tensions. This kind of relaxation gives a climactic quality to bar 40. But it comes too early. It seems unearned and thus arbitrary. Moreover, the emphasis on D is carried by a themelike motif. Listeners must wonder whether they are not hearing a second theme, not only in the "wrong" key, but also too soon both in the sense that a relaxing subdominant is not yet viable and also in the sense that D has not been adequately tonicized. The relief experienced when the themelike motif is treated as a canon, not as a paired subphrase, and D is abandoned and replaced by the dominant of F in bar 44, revealing that the D material is not the second theme after all, is a component of the climax characterizing the end of the bridge (bars 44–47).

(iii) The Double Recapitulation

Beethoven does not direct that his exposition be repeated (repeat signs appear around 83% of the 1824–26 expositions). Omitting the repeat of the exposition is closely related to recapitulating it twice. Having presented his musical material only once before the development, Beethoven can present it twice afterwards without undue redundancy, especially as the series of tonalities are different in all three:

exposition:

a	– d	– F
bars 1–28	40–43	44–74

first recapitulation:

e	– a	– C
bars 119–33	151–54	155–88

second recapitulation:

a	– a	– a
bars 193–214	215–22	223–30

FIGURE 46
Beethoven, Quartet, Op. 132/i

Analysts[3] worry about calling bars 119–192 a recapitulation for two reasons. First, it is said to begin too soon; material from only one source in the exposition has been developed (the fact that 79% of the 1824–26 developments derive their material from more than one part of the exposition supports this argument). Yet the material between the exposition and the first recapitulation is longer relative to the exposition than are 62% of the 1824–26 developments, and this datum suggests that Beethoven's audience would not have heard a recapitulation beginning in bar 119 as "too soon" at all. Moreover, Beethoven has, by bar 119, articulated three distinct gestures including a plausible retransition (bars 75–91, 92–102 and 103–18; see Figure 46). Both these features make the listener ready for the recapitulation.

The second and more significant cause for worrying about the term "recapitulation" for bars 119–92 is that the themes are not reviewed in the tonic. It is not particularly troublesome (though it is rare) for the first theme not to be recapitulated in the tonic; it at least was presented in the tonic in the exposition. But for the second not to be recapitulated in the tonic seems to contradict the very purpose of the recapitulation, which is, as Rosen puts it, to resolve the exposition's tonal contrast by presenting in the tonic the main material that the exposition has presented in keys other than the tonic.[4] The actual practice of Viennese composers during Beethoven's time was, however, not so absolutely uniform as Rosen implies: 2% of the 1795–1826 themes are recapitulated in a key other than the tonic, 1% are not recapitulated at all, and another 5% recapitulate the first part of the second theme in a non-tonic key, then move to the tonic for the rest of the second theme reprise. In none of these 8% is the second theme presented elsewhere (in the development or coda) in the tonic and thereby "resolved," nor is it a straightforward variation of the first theme (for if it were, the second theme statement in a non-tonic key would not require a resolution). Nevertheless, it is the case that a harmonic pattern of Beethoven's bars 119–92 is not analogous to that in most recapitulations.

Although the analogy between Beethoven's "first recapitulation" and conventional 1824–26 recapitulations is flawed, this section is even less analogous to the "false recapitulations" that sometimes occur within development sections. The review of themes in bars 119–92 is so extended and so similar to the exposition, and a development section that went from bar 75 to bar 192 would be so long that appeal to this model would obscure more than it would illumine.

Perhaps the analogy that best illumines bars 119–92 is their similarity to the procedure of repeating the development-recapitulation.

While this procedure is almost unheard of today, it was not completely forgotten in the early nineteenth century. Beethoven uses it in the Finale of his Op. 57 Piano Sonata (1804–05). Of the sonata movements published in Vienna during 1815-23, 5% direct that the development-recapitulation be repeated, and in another 2% the publisher has put a repeat sign at the beginning of the development but has carelessly omitted one at the end of the movement. In 1824–26, the repeat of the development-recapitulation is not unequivocally directed in any of the pieces studied, but 7% have the repeat sign at the beginning of the development (:‖:) and none at the end of the movement. Just as publishers were sloppy about marking the repeat, so also performers were no doubt careless about heeding the direction.

Nevertheless, the procedure existed. Beethoven's bars 119–92 appeal to this model, though they depart from it in two ways. First, the development is not repeated; the music moves directly from the recapitulation closing (bars 177–192 [= bars 62–74] to the second recapitulation. Not repeating the development between the recapitulations, Beethoven can write a second development after the second recapitulation (namely the coda) without undue redundancy.

Second, the second recapitulation varies the first one. The first recapitulation repeats the entire theme and the bridge without any abbreviation (Beethoven is being unconventional: while 76% of the 1824–26 first phrases and 50% of the second phrases are not shortened in the recapitulation, and 48% of the reprise bridges are as long as or longer than their exposition counterpart, nevertheless only 21% resemble Beethoven's first recapitulation in not shortening something in the first half of the reprise). In this respect, the second recapitulation is altogether different. It completely obliterates phrase pairing in the first theme (see bars 199–212 in Figure 51), it abbreviates the bridge (compare bars 32–48 with 215–23), and it truncates the second theme by allowing a return of the first theme and the onset of the coda to displace the last three bars of the second theme (while bars 224–31 correspond to bars 49–56, bars 232–34 deviate from bars 57–59; see Figures 45, 47a and 48). The second recapitulation deviates thematically from the usual recapitulation as much as the first deviates harmonically.

Writing two recapitulations is an ingeniously deft way to deal with the exposition's anomalous key scheme (a,d, and F, horizontalizing the D minor triad). In the first recapitulation, the first theme reprise dwells on E, and the second theme reprise is in C; the key which the listener expected for the second theme in the exposition is in fact used for the second theme in the first recapitulaion. Thus the three tonal centers of the first recapitulation (e - a - C) horizontalize the A-minor triad and contribute significantly to the tonal stability of the movement as a whole.

In short, the harmonic peculiarities of the first recapitulation respond to the harmonic irregularities of the exposition. Reviewing all the themes without yet stating the second theme in the tonic summons a second recapitulation, which to avoid redundancy, needs to be abbreviated at all points except the second theme.

Although the first recapitulation is exactly as long as the exposition, the proportions are different. The front-heaviness characterizing the exposition is eased, for the first part is shortened by omitting the slow introduction and the second part is lengthened by extending the closing gesture that rounds out the paired phrases of the second theme (compare bars 57–62 in Figure 47a with 168–77 in Figure 47b), and by tacking on transitional material (bars 189–92) before the second recapitulation begins. Consequently, the 65:35 proportions in the exposition (almost 2:1) become 50:45 (5:4) in the first reprise.

FIGURE 47
Beethoven, Quartet, Op. 132/i

a)

Lengthening the second theme closing is particularly important because the ten bars of this closing build, in two waves (bars 168–71 and
172–77), an intensity that peaks in the *fortissimo* of bar 177 and that is
much stronger than the intensity culminating at the corresponding
place in the exposition (bar 62). The climax in the second part of this
recapitulation (bar 177) is consequently as strong as the climaxes in
its first part (at bars 151 and 158–59). In the exposition, the climax in
the first part overbalances that in the second part. Since the climaxes
in the two parts of the first recapitulation balance one another and the
lengths nearly do, the greater stability of the second theme becomes
decisive, and bars 119–92 are heard as a stable, end-accented pair of
groups.

b)

FIGURE 48
Beethoven, Quartet, Op. 132/i

The second recapitulation carries forward a resolution of the tensions generated in the exposition by the equivocal relationship of its parts. First, the second theme is finally presented in the tonic. Second, the proportions of the two parts are 31:41 (almost 3:4), so that the front-heaviness of the exposition, which is eased in the first recapitulation, is now set aside in favor of a decisively end-heavy group. Third, the stronger climax appears in the second part. The climaxes projected in the first part of the second reprise (bars 214 and 222) are somewhat weaker than their counterparts in the exposition bridge (bars 40 and 47) and first reprise bridge (bars 151 and 158) because in the latter two cases, the harmony has moved to the subdominant, thereby relaxing tension, while in the second reprise the themelike material for the canon is in the same key (a) as the first theme. The climax projected in the second part of the second reprise is stronger, for the coda is decisively climactic: it is full of chromaticisms and *sforzandi*. It has twice as much persistent sixteenth-note motion as the first recapitulation closing, and the only sustained *fortissimo* (bars 247–48) in the movement. See Figure 48. In all these ways, the coda releases the movement's pent-up energies and serves as its climax.

Thus the movement as a whole consists of the following progression. In the first section (exposition), the first part (first-theme-plus-bridge) is longer and more climactic than the second (second-theme-plus-exposition-closing), yet the material in the second is basically stabler. In the first recapitulation, the two parts are almost equally long and equally climactic, and the material is, again, stabler in the second part. In the third section, the second part is longer than the first, and the climax shifts unequivocally to the second part. This linear, end-directing, progressive resolution of one of the exposition's anomalies supports and is supported by the progressive resolution of its harmonies: The middle section puts the themelike motif of the bridge's canon into the tonic and the second theme into the key that was expected for it in the exposition, and the third section uses the tonic for all the themes.

(2) The Center-controlled Shape

At the same time that the movement progressively resolves the exposition's internal inconsistencies, other conspicuous features assert themselves that play no part in this dynamic process. These features work together to create a more static form whose shape is controlled by the nature of its large central section.

The movement is divided into three principal sections by its strongest and virtually identical articulations. These occur at the end of the exposition and the end of the first recapitulation. As Figure 49 indicates, the first and last of these sections are equally long, and the middle section is strikingly longer.

Its greater length by itself does not make it the center of gravity. Indeed, the dynamic process described above has its focus in the final section, in spite of the proportions of the sections. Rather, the middle section is the focus of a second process because of the way it responds to still another anomaly in the first section, namely, the exposition's weak contrasts between paired and non-paired material.

FIGURE 49
Proportions and Shape of Beethoven, Quartet, Op. 132/i

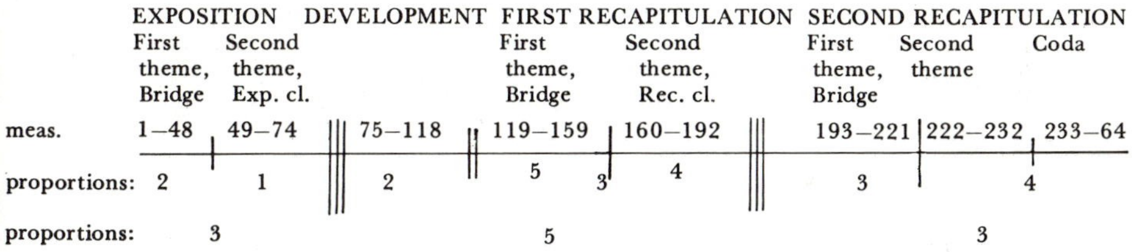

	EXPOSITION	DEVELOPMENT	FIRST RECAPITULATION	SECOND RECAPITULATION
	First theme, Bridge	Second theme, Exp. cl.		First theme, Bridge	Second theme, Rec. cl.		First theme, Bridge	Second theme	Coda
meas.	1–48	49–74	‖‖ 75–118 ‖	119–159	160–192 ‖‖	193–221	222–232	233–64
proportions:	2	1	‖‖ 2 ‖	5 3	4 ‖‖	3	4
proportions:	3		5	3

(i) The Weak Contrasts within the First Section

The contrast of paired to non-paired material is essential and normative to the sonata-allegro process of Beethoven's time. The introduction (if there is one), bridge, closing, development and coda typically are not structured by paired phrases, while the first and second themes invariably consist of paired phrases, each phrase often comprising a pair of subphrases. In fact, it is the appearance of a second set of paired phrases in a new key that defines the second theme. The alternation of paired with non-paired material, the latter usually forming a group with the paired material that precedes it, creates a rhythm that gives the movement its shape. In each movement, this organization is particularized by the differing strengths of the articulations, the varying degrees of forward thrust generated in each section and the varying degrees of finality characterizing the ends of sections.

Much of what makes the shape of Op. 132/i distinctive is the result of weakening the contrast between the paired phrases and the mate-

FIGURE 50
Beethoven, Quartet, Op. 132/i

rial intervening between the paired-phrases sections. Beethoven softens this differentiation by disguising the points at which the first theme's subphrases begin and end, by weakening the bond that pairs the first theme's first subphrase to the second, by masking the end of the second theme paired subphrases and the beginning of the exposition closing, and by using themelike material within the bridge.

The beginning of the first theme is disguised by a false start to the first subphrase. The introduction seems to end on the downbeat of bar 11 (see Figure 50), for the motif struck up by the cello on the second beat of that bar is clearly themelike. But at the end of the first subphrase (bar 16), the listener recognizes that the subphrase in fact consists of the melody played by the first violin in bars 13–16, that it divides itself symmetrically into two units, each with two downbeats, and that bars 11–12 in the cello stand outside this subphrase. Alternatively, one could hear the cello in bar 11 as the beginning of a five-downbeat group, but such a group sounds less like a subphrase summoning a paired subphrase than does a group consisting of a false start plus a four-bar unit.

Beethoven disguises the end of the first subphrase by extending it sequentially. There are ways of expanding a subphrase that enable listeners clearly to distinguish between the subphrase and its expansion; for example, when a subphrase is extended by ending it first with a false cadence and then a couple of bars later with a half or full cadence, they hear both where the subphrase "ought" to end (if it is to match the length of its pair) and where the expanded subphrase in fact ends. Expanding a subphrase by a sequential repetition of its last part is rarely used (only 4% of the 1815–23 and none of the 1824–26 first themes studied have it), and, more than any other means of expanding a subphrase, sequential repetition makes it hard for listeners to distinquish between the subphrase and its extension.

The second subphrase (bars 23–26) is not preceded by a false start, but having heard a false start to its pair, the listener does not at first know whether the second violin and cello in bar 23 are another false start or the actual beginning of the second subphrase. The ending of the second subphrase is disguised in that this subphrase, like its pair, is extended, and the extension flows without a cadential break into the bridge. There is no point at which one can say that the bridge begins; but while hearing bar 31, one is aware that a transition is underway.

In addition to disguising the beginning and ending of subphrases, Beethoven also softens the differentiation between paired and nonpaired material by weakening the bond between the first and second subphrases in the first theme. The weaker this bond, the more likely the listener is to hear the subphrases as merely successive and not paired. By sequentially extending the first subphrase and then recalling the introductory material for two bars, Beethoven puts so much material between the four-bar subphrases that it is difficult to hear the first as related to the second.

The second theme's beginning is clear and undisguised, as is the end of its first subphrase (bar 52; see Figure 45). Listeners realize that the paired subphrase ends in bar 56, but because the dominant persists in the bass, they also realize that the subphrase is extended. This expansion gradually acquires the character of a second theme closing (see Figure 47a). While the expansion of the second theme in many sonatas of the time serves the function of a second theme closing, listeners are not ready for such a closing in bar 57. Of the 1824–26 second themes, 83% have a pair of phrases, each of which consists of a pair of subphrases, and only 10% have, as Op. 132/i has, only a single pair of subphrases. Moreover, Beethoven's first theme occupies twenty bars, and one therefore does not expect the second theme paired material to cease after only eight bars. For these two reasons, the listener is not aware that paired phrasing has been left behind until many bars later.

The cadential formula articulated by the second theme closing is complete in bar 62. Bar 63 is analogous to exposition closing in other movements in that it alludes to the beginning of the piece (compare it to bar 9). But the onset of Beethoven's exposition closing is also disguised: the second theme closing ends on a first-inversion, not root-position, chord (first beat, bar 62), and the sixteenth notes in the three lower parts deny the cadence its rest.

Finally, the appearance of a themelike gesture within the bridge at bars 41–44 (Figure 45) disminishes the contrast between paired and non-paired material. Although this gesture, it turns out, is treated as a canon and not as a paired phrase, it is confusing to hear this sort of material within the bridge.

It would be wrong, however, to infer that Beethoven intended the listener to hear no differentiation at all between paired and non-paired material. Because every sonata-allegro movement with which his audiences were acquainted featured such an alternation, they surely expected to hear paired phrases and an alternation of paired with non-paired material. These expectations were so strong, one may suppose, that he could fulfill them through fairly weak phrase linking and understated contrasts.

In the first theme, the expectation is met in three ways. First, the shape of the melody that appears in bars 13–16 seems themelike in contrast to the melodically amorphous introduction. The amorphous shape of the introduction has created pressure toward a themelike melodic contour, and the rhapsodic figure (bars 9–10) that extends the introduction has increased this pressure sufficiently that even the false start of the first subphrase, deliberately confusing though it is, by no means obliterates the opposition between the non-paired material of 1–12 and the themelike material of what seems by contrast to be the movement's first subphrase.

Second, the six-bar gesture from the upbeat to bar 17 through the downbeat of bar 22 (see Figure 50) not only functions to separate the two four-bar subphrases, making it difficult to hear the two as related, but also has the opposite effect: forward thrust has been weakly engendered in bar 16 (second beat), as the melody of the first subphrase ends on the third of the chord; the roughly sequential character of bars 16–18 and the rising arpeggio (E - A - C) articulated by bars 17–21 intensify this thrust. The stronger the forward push, the stronger the sense that bars 23–26 are the goal of that forward movement and that the subphrases are paired.

Third, the listener's awareness that bars 13–16 and 23–26 are paired subphrases which precipitate out of the flux of bars 1–26 is supported by the regular recurrence of the same rhythmic pattern:

$$ | \; \flat \; \flat\flat\flat \; \flat \; \flat\flat\flat \; | \; \flat\flat \; \sim . $$

This pattern occurs twice in each subphrase. The repetition has three effects: it divides each subphrase into two parts, it links the two parts together so that they form a single unit, and it helps pair the two subphrases to each other. The melodies of the two subphrases are also identical, and this linking has the same effect. Using the same melodic or rhythmic pattern either to divide and join the parts of a subphrase or to help relate two subphrases to one another is typical of the 1824–26 paired phrases. But it is somewhat unusual to find both used within a single set of paired phrases: only 38% of the 1824–26 first themes have rhythmic or melodic linkings both within a subphrase and across subphrases. The appearance of both types in Beethoven's first theme has the effect, however, not of novelty, but of countering to some extent the forces weakening the contrast of paired and non-paired material so that the listener will at least dimly hear the customary opposition in spite of the forces contradicting it.

(ii) The Strong Contrast within the Second Section

Within the exposition as a whole, the conventional distinction between paired and non-paired materials has been maintained, but it is unconventionally weak. The exposition comes close to being a single, undifferentiated gesture, which would be anomalous. The caesura separating it from the development (bars 74–75; Figure 46) is by no means as strongly marked as it is in many of the 1795–1826 sonatas, but it is so much clearer than any of the articulations within the exposition that it both unequivocally identifies the development as the beginning of a new section and also enhances the sense that the exposition is a single gesture.

Much the same thing must be said of the similar articulation separating the first from the second recapitulation (bars 191–92; Figure 51). This caesura is also so strong, compared to the caesuras within either recapitulation, that the two recapitulations must be heard as separate groups. The various abbreviations and omissions within the second recapitulation, the amalgamation of its first theme with the bridge and its second theme with the coda and its persistent use of A minor make this final section an even more undifferentiated gesture than the exposition.

FIGURE 51
Beethoven, Quartet, Op. 132/i

The beginning of the first recapitulation is clearly marked, and this articulation is only slightly weaker than the caesuras at the beginning of the development and the beginning of the second recapitulation. Discontinuity on the note-to-note level is about the same at all three points. But discontinuity on the section-to-section level is much less in the case of the caesura at the onset of the first recapitulation because the degree of forward thrust jumping the gap is higher here than it is at the other two caesuras. As the following paragraphs will indicate, this difference between the onset of the first recapitulation, on the one hand, and the other two of the movement's three principal points of articulation, on the other, is crucial in shaping the movement: it is critical both to the strong contrast of non-paired to paired material within the second section and to the contrast of weakly differentiated material in section one to clearly differentiated material in section two.

As a generator of forward thrust, the exposition is equivocal. Paying attention to one set of features, one hears it as a stable gesture whose ending has only the forward thrust that is generated by closing in a key different from the one in which it began. Paying attention to another set of features, one hears a wobbly gesture that pushes toward a completion beyond its own ending. A "tone of insecurity," As Kerman puts it, [5] characterizes its final cadence, for in bar 74 (Figure 46) the terminal F major chord is delayed a beat, it is played unexpectedly *piano* and it introduces a lowered seventh (E-flat), eliding the tonic of F with the dominant of B-flat. This chord, vacillating between closure and openness, is a tidy synecdoche for the exposition as a whole.

The development, however, is unequivocally dynamic. Its process of generating energy has three peaks, each of them a measure of four widely spaced quarter-note hammer blows (bars 91, 102 and 118; see Figure 46). Although the development is unified by the pervasive first theme motif, the similarity of these three measures divides the process into three waves and coordinates their cumulative effect. The first surge ends in bar 91. The meaningless silence in bar 92 rejects this surge, but the second wave builds to a higher peak (bar 102). These two waves generate enormous pressure into the restransition, which in turn intensifies the push forward. During the first two waves of the development, the energy is out of control in the sense that one cannot foresee the particularities of the event — when will it come to pass? what key will it be in? what motif will carry it? — that will channel the energy into a definite and responsive form. The retransition gets its name from the fact that, during it, the pressure focuses itself toward a specific goal, the recapitulation in E minor.

Thus the development unequivocally forms a pair with the first recapitulation. Analogous to Classic paired phrases, the two groups are clearly separated, yet also clearly bound together because forward thrust jumps the separating gap and the second group ends more stably than the first.

The shape of the middle section of the movement (that is, the development plus the first reprise) is far more sharply defined and definite than that of the other two. Its two parts unambiguously form a pair. The paired group is stable not only because the second part ends so much more stably than the first part, but also because the second is much longer than the first part. As Figure 49 indicates, the length of the development is only two-thirds that of the first recapitulation.

(iii) The Contrast between Sections One and Two

The middle section responds to the exposition's anomalously weak differentiation between paired and non-paired material in two ways. First, the three waves of the development are unequivocally non-paired material and make an unmistakable contrast with even the disguised pairings of the first recapitulation. The differentiation which is only adumbrated in the exposition here takes place in broad daylight. Second, the middle section strongly pairs its first part (the development) to its second part (the first recapitulation), and this clear pairing contrasts to the exposition, which as a single, weakly differentiated gesture only confusedly projects its internal pairings. In short, just as the first recapitulation, in contrast to the development, consists of paired material, so on a higher level the development-plus-first-recapitulation as a whole is comprised of paired material, in contrast to the exposition. Both contrasts respond to the weak differentiation between paired and non-paired material in the exposition. Both contrasts concretize an objective to which the exposition points.

While the middle section in these two ways resolves one of the critical tensions set up in the exposition, the third section (that is, the second recapitulation) does nothing to further this resolution. In fact, it lapses into a degree of non-differentiation greater than that in the first section. Thus, the first two sections make a goal-directed group, but no end-directed relationship between the second and third sections is actualized. The movement as a whole has its focus in its center. The conspicuously greater length of the middle section strengthens its power to function as the movement's focus.

(3) Two Shapes Compounding the Ambiguity of the Temporal Process

In the exposition the differentiation between paired and non-paired material both does and does not happen. This equivocation projects the image of a temporal process in which past and present events summon a particular future, but this future both does and does not happen. The lack of clear differentiation makes each new present seem not to fulfill its past and not to be the future summoned by the past.

A musical flow in which no differentiation at all occurs has no points of arrival. A single subphrase, for example, has no arrivals within itself. Unless an exposition as a whole has some sort of internal differentiation analogous to the difference between two phrases that are paired to each other, its process is analogous to that of a single subphrase. Like an isolated subphrase, such an exposition or movement can not exemplify the process in which a decision is made that would cut the present off from the past; it cannot suggest a present in which something fresh and in some sense new is happening. Each successive present responds to its past only in that it extends it and prolongs its struggle to actualize a goal. If the entire temporal process is an undifferentiated flux, the actualization of fulfillment within that flow is impossible. If there is fulfillment, it would have to be outside the temporal process. If no fulfillment within the temporal process is possible, the self cannot take responsibility for what happens. The self undergoes temporal experience, but can not direct or shape it.

Supposing that Beethoven's exposition were completely undifferentiated, one might simply hear the next section, which is clearly distinct from it, as the actualization of its goal. The exposition as a whole might evoke a future, and one might hear the next section as the concrete occurrence of that future. The process would be hard to follow because of the length of the summoning section, but it would be no more problematic than any pair of phrases. But Beethoven's exposition is not completely undifferentiated. There is just enough suggestion of a subphrase coming into being as a response to a prior subphrase, and of a second part answering the summons of a first part, that one dimly senses an image of the kind of temporality in which a deciding agent responds to the past, shapes the future and actualizes itself. The temporal process associated with Classic sonata-allegro movements is adumbrated; it is not clearly articulated, nor is it completely abrogated. Because the differentiation between paired and non-paired material is suggested, one is aware of the sonata-allegro process and its temporality, but because it is weak, the happening of summoned events seems sketchy. One is not sure whether they are actually taking place or whether they only seem to take place. As the exposition unfolds, the music both continues and extends the past and also seems to suggest what fulfillment would be like if it were actual, as perhaps it already is.

The equivocation between continuing and beginning reminds one of the Trio, Op. 1/2/i, and the difference between that movement and Op. 132/i illumines the latter. In 1/2/i, gestures are ambiguous as they occur, for they seem to suggest both the beginning of a fresh event and the continuing of an event already in motion, but, a few bars later, one retrospectively realizes that in fact a new gesture has begun. An event occurs, suggesting the process of making a decision — though a decision so controlled by the past that it seems at first to be no more than a continuation of the past. In 132/i, however, the differentiation between paired and non-paired material is weak all the way through the exposition, so that the listener is never sure (until the development) whether an event — a past — or a future-oriented event — is taking place, has taken place or is about to take place.

This very equivocation establishes as a goal the removal of such ambiguity, and the focal power of the central section resides in the fact that it is unambiguous in precisely the way that the first section is equivocal. The tortuous struggle to separate past from future such that a fulfillment will precipitate out of what would otherwise be an undifferentiated temporal flux succeeds. The first recapitulation objectifies the completion toward which the development pushes, and this objectification in turn objectifies the separation of the future from the past and of actual fulfillment from imagined or hoped for fulfillment. Without such objectified separation the temporal process would consist of a seething succession of transformations, but it would actualize no goals. The self involved in this process would undergo experience, but would not shape it.

The fact that the third section lapses from this objectification into a nearly undifferentiated flow does not attenuate the achievement of the central section, nor impugn the possibility that fulfillment can be actual. Its effect is to reintroduce and intensify the difficulty, already experienced in the exposition, of separating a fulfilling future from a struggling past. Slipping back into non-differentiation makes one feel that while concrete fulfillments are possible, they do not always characterize the temporal process. The contrast between the second and third sections gives the achievement of the second section a sharper profile. The remarkable distinction between the degree of differentiation in the second section and that in the third makes the temporal process in which a fulfillment actually and clearly takes place seem remarkable, unusual and even extraordinary. It is as though the first and third sections are the image of ordinary circumstances in which one cannot expect the future unambiguously to fulfill the past and in which the self more undergoes than shapes experience.

But clearly the events that do more completely fulfill their past become the focus of the temporal process. Temporality may alternately consist of a future that both does and does not actualize the past's goals and a future that unequivocally realizes the objectives pursued by the past, but all equivocally fulfilling processes are experienced in relationship to that rare and remarkable process in which goals are unequivocally actualized. Either equivocal fulfillments look forward to an unequivocal one and press toward it — as the first section of Op. 132/i does in relation to the second section — or they look backward to it and subordinate their own hazy meaningfulness to the meaning that has already been established — as does the third section of Op. 132/i.

This temporality is obviously not one in which heroism makes sense, and the music has no heroic connotations. Instead of hearing Everyman masquerading as a hero, as we do in the "Archduke" Trio and the "Hammerklavier" Sonata, we hear Everyman undergoing his — or her, as it now makes sense to say, for while heroes are traditionally masculine, the persona of processes like the one in 132/i is not — impotence to control the temporal process, yet persistently centering the understanding of temporality on the segments when his or her efforts are effective. In the kind of temporality exemplified by the "Archduke" and the "Hammerklavier," the self can evidently identify itself only with events that it shapes; but in the temporality exemplified by the middle-focused process of Op. 132/i, the self is just as much what it undergoes when an occurrence extends its past as it is what it expresses itself to be when it shapes a future by actualizing its own unique goals.

Although the temporal process projected by the middle-focused shape has a dynamic segment, as a whole it is neither dynamic nor static. In some respects it moves ahead; in some respects it gets to where it has been moving; in some respects it does not get to its goal; in some respects it guides its move ahead by looking backward. Such a temporal process is fundamentally incompatible with the other process through which the movement leads the listener — a process with an end-directed shape.

As indicated in section (1) above, the movement's end-directed shape consists of the way the exposition's proportions and placements of climaxes contradict the comparative stability of the second theme and the way the two recapitulations successively resolve this anomaly. The temporal process projected by the contradictory aspects of the exposition is confused. To the extent that the second theme is stable relative to the first theme, listening to the exposition unfold gives one the sense of moving from a past to a fresh and responsive future. The free decision that shapes this process and gives the future its newness seems to be future-oriented. But because the first theme plus bridge is so much longer and more climactic than the second theme plus closing, one also feels while listening to the latter part that the focal event has already taken place and that the second theme and exposition closing are backward looking. These aspects of the exposition's shape suggest that the decision involved in the process of moving from the past to a responsive future is a decision to perpetutate the status quo rather than to create something genuinely fresh and unique.

Thus the anomalies within the exposition suggest two contradictory ways of experiencing temporality. The comparatively stable second theme projects one image of the way a person experiences the contrast between past and future, and the proportions and climaxes in the exposition project a contradictory image. In both images, the temporal process involves a decision that, together with the past, shapes the realizations that articulate temporality. But in the one, this decision seems to be guided by the self's understanding of itself as radically particular, and its attempts to actualize itself intend to create a future that is as unique as it is. In the other, the decision seems to be guided by a self that, as Heidegger would say, is lost in the "they-self," does not understand itself as radically particular, and seeks a future that re-concretizes already established routines. The uncertainty produced by the wobble between originality and routine evokes a desire to create a new temporality that is unambiguously future-oriented, and the second and third sections of the movement, as they progressively resolve the exposition's anomalies, respond affirmatively.

The ambiguities which generate the middle-focused shape are very different from those which generate the end-directed shape. It is tempting to suppose that the one reinforces the other. As a matter of fact, however, the one kind of ambiguity has more the effect of obscuring than of supporting the other kind. The ambiguity generating the middle-focused shape is the equivocal differentiation between paired and non-paired material. The instance of this ambiguity that bears particularly on the ambiguity generating the end-directed shape occurs at the beginning of the second theme. The caesura between the bridge and the second theme is clear enough, but because of the proximity of the themelike material of the bridge's canon to the second theme, the differentiation between paired and non-paired material is equivocal. This lack of clarity makes it hard for the listener to know whether the caesura at the beginning of the second theme has any structural significance, and if it does not, then the anomaly created by the exposition's proportions and climaxes, on the one hand, and the comparative stability of its themes, on the other, simply disappears. That is, to the extent that the material is undifferentiated, the temporal process is an undifferentiated flux in which actualizing fulfillment is impossible. If the goal toward which the first theme plus bridge is working does not take place in the second theme plus closing, as the lack of clear differentiation suggests that it does not, then the question as to whether the fulfillment of that goal is original or routine is simply undercut. Only as the development plus first recapitulation makes a sharper contrast between paired and non-paired material does the resolution of the anomalous relation of the two themes clearly emerge as a goal. During the exposition, there is just enough differentiation between paired and non-paired material that one dimly senses the anomalous relation of the two themes, but because the differentiation is persistently equivocal throughout the exposition, one does not feel capable of identifying this anomaly. All things considered, the exposition creates a way of experiencing the contrast between past and future in which one wants to work toward a fulfilling future but has no clear idea of what would count for fulfillment. Listening to the exposition is like sensing that one has a problem and feels a tension, but does not know at all precisely what it is. Only as the development plus first recapitulation makes a sharper contrast between paired and non-paired material does the resolution of the anomalous relation of the two themes clearly emerge as a goal.

   Just as it is tempting, but wrong, to suppose that the two kinds of ambiguity reinforce one another, so it is also easy, but misleading, to assume that the end-directed shape is more basic than the middle-focused one. In particular, one who begins listening to the piece with the prior conviction that the future can actualize the present's goals will not want to hear the progression from weakly to strongly differentiated material as constituting a middle-focused shape. This shape is propelled by an equivocation that denies the prior conviction, and so this listener will want to regard this progression as part of the end-directed shape. Such a hearing will regard the middle section as the resolution of one of the tensions created by the exposition, while other objectives set up in the first section must await the third section for their final completion. Contradicting this hearing, the middle section insists on itself through its considerable length and stability. Hearing it as only a step toward a completion ignores these features. It also ignores the way the third section not only does not further the differentiation between paired and non-paired material heard in the second section, but also fails even to sustain that resolution at the same level as the second section.

It is just as impossible, or willful, to hear the end-directed shape as subordinate to the middle-focused one. Had Beethoven's end-directed shape been perfunctory in any way, it might have been overbalanced by the more unusual middle-focused one. A purposive march to fulfillment is, after all, one which other sonata-allegro movements by Beethoven and Classic composers generally have made familiar, and the attention of the listener who is acquainted with numerous instances of the Classic process might have been pulled to the more extraordinary shape, which demands more of the listener. Or perhaps listeners might have found the familiar shape so comfortable that they might have ignored the middle-focused shape and its tensions as well as the tension between the two shapes. In any case, Op. 132/i stands out from the others in that the discontinuities it risks and overcomes are unprecedented in the history of music. It confirms the temporal process projected by other sonata forms in the sense that in it fulfillment happens in the face of the most profoundly disturbing discontinuities. Had this shape been generated in a more conventional way, no matter how strong the thrust to the end nor how brilliant its execution, this process and the self as a deciding and shaping agent that it suggests would have been less significant than the middle-focused process and the duality of experience — what happens is both shaped and undergone by the self — that it exemplifies. A perfunctory end-directed shape would have contributed to the first pole of this duality, but might not have served as a counterweight to the middle-focused process as a whole nor contradicted the duality. But because the end-directed process risks unprecedented discontinuities, establishes fundamentally new goals, and achieves its objectives progressively in the altogether unique double recapitulation, it sustains its temporal process — in which the concept of a moral self is viable — just as convincingly as the middle-oriented shape contradicts it and attenuates the validity of this concept.

In the end, all the listener can do is to accept the contradiction that the temporal process involves both an equivocal and an unambiguous march to completion. In Op. 90/i, aspects of two distinct shapes support and reinforce one another without vitiating their separateness, but in Op. 132/i, nothing happens that would suggest that its two shapes are only apparently contradictory. Nothing happens that would transcend the contradiction and establish a new image of the temporal process. Listeners are called upon to live simultaneously two temporalities, and they are given no hope of making this process rational either to those who adopt Newtonian common sense or to those who see the self as a reasoning and deciding agent.

The temporal process exemplified by the movement can be clarified by comparing it to Heidegger's depiction of temporality. In *Being and Time*, Heidegger talks about two temporalities. Human existence, he says, "is always coming towards,"[6] but what it is coming towards is inconstant. In authentic temporality, an entity existing in the human way of existing anticipates its own radical particularity that is to be lost when it dies. In the other temporality, what is lived towards is more like the goals of people in general: one is coming towards what a vague someone, or everyone, ought to be, and is becoming a self that understands itself in terms of that with which it is concerned. The one temporality is suggested in the sentence, "I am who I am becoming," which the other kind of future rejects as empirically vague. The other temporality is suggested in the sentence, "I am what I shall do," which the authentic future rejects as losing oneself in one's concerns — those possible or urgent or even indispensable (by some standard extrinsic to authentic human existence) activities in which one submerges oneself most of the time.[7]

Heidegger's analysis is puzzling, initially, in the following way: How can a person living toward his or her own uniqueness ever lapse from that temporality into an inauthentic one, and how can one living toward an inauthentic future ever move out of that way of being? The question gets its point from the fact that intrinsic to each form of the future is a fundamental rejection of the other. It seems irrational to say that everyone alternates between the two temporalities, for there cannot possibly be a dynamic that would drive a person from either one to the other. It would be inconsistent with Heidegger's basic assumptions to suppose that the two are merely different manifestations of some deeper self to which the distinction does not apply.

A possible response to the puzzle is to remember that Heidegger is describing the structure of human existence, not drawing generalizations from observations of concrete human behavior and attitudes. Authentic and inauthentic temporality describe structures that determine possibilities. Heidegger seems to be saying that to exist in the human way necessarily involves the possibility of both kinds of futures. On the one hand, it necessarily involves being in the world and the concomitant temptation to fall into the world (that is, understand oneself in its terms and be dominated by the they-self), a temptation to which a person inevitably (though perhaps not necessarily) succumbs. On the other hand, the phenomenon of conscience attests to the fact that a person is continuously summoned to itself; it is continuously called out of its lostness in the they-self, and this call does not come from God or any absolute code extrinsic to itself — indeed it comes from nowhere but itself. The phenomenon of conscience and the very fact that humans exert energy in hiding from its call are indications that a person both always has the possibility of authentic existence and also in some sense always already does exist authentically.[8]

Heidegger seems to be suggesting that a concrete person is an undifferentiated blend of authenticity and inauthenticity. The two structures are both present, and each of them is an abstraction from what is concretely actual. The concrete actualizations of the two possibilities are so complexly intertwined that they cannot be sorted out, and one is left with the conclusion that both of them characterize concrete persons as well as the set of human possibilities. In short, everyone lives both temporalities.[9]

The point of mentioning Heidegger in connection with Beethoven's Quartet, Op. 132/i, is not to suggest that one of its temporal processes corresponds to what Heidegger calls authentic temporality and the other to inauthentic temporality. Instead, the point is simply that Heidegger understands the concrete human experience of the contrast between past, present and future as an experience that is irreducibly complex, and Beethoven's movement exemplifies such an irreducibly complex process. The process which the one depicts and the other exemplifies is irreducibly complex in the sense that it consists of two contradictory ways of experiencing the contrast, and neither one can be reduced to a form of the other, neither can be subordinated to the other, nor can both of them be reduced to forms of some logically prior understanding of the contrast. Each of the incompatible ways makes at least some sense by itself, but each is an abstraction from concrete experience in which the two are interwoven, each challenging the validity of the other, but neither supplanting the other. The Op., 59/1/i vision of a future-oriented inner self that is completely integrated with a past-oriented|public self has faded away: while Op. 59/1/i seems to suggest that the future-orientation of authentic temporality can coincide with the past-orientation of inauthentic temporality, Op. 132/i seems to suggest that fragmentation is in fact unavoidable and perhaps even ultimate.

Both the Quartet, Op. 132/i, and the Sonata, Op. 90/i, have two disparate shapes. The difference between the Quartet, in which disparate shapes contradict each other, and the Sonata, in which disparate shapes reinforce one another, corresponds to the difference between Heidegger and his teacher, Edmund Husserl. In his *Cartesian Meditations* (1931), Husserl analyzes the structure of consciousness and tries to show that consciousness always and necessarily involves an object; to be conscious is to be conscious of something.[10] And both the subject that is conscious and the object of which the subject is conscious have a temporal structure. The object of consciousness is temporal in the sense that that of which one is conscious is more than the object of a single perception or the stimulus of an isolated sensation, for it always involves synthesizing that perception with remembered perceptions and expected or hoped for perceptions. That of which one is conscious is always more than one is perceiving in a given moment.[11] The present perception of a table, for instance, is synthesized with remembered perceptions of that table seen from a slightly or greatly different angle, in more or less light, and so on, and with perceptions that one has in fact never had but would expect to have. The object of consciousness is a temporal object because it includes the object of past and future perceptions which are identified with a present perception and at the same time distiguished from each other and from the stimulus of the present sensation. The object of consciousness is the synthesis of past perceptions *as past* and of future ones *as future*.[12] If consciousness did not make such a distinction among present, recollected and anticipated perceptions, its present object would be totally dissociated from other objects (and would be a totally different object from the synthesized objects of which one is in fact conscious). In the absence of some kind of association between and temporal distinction among a present and other perceptions, one's total world would consist of that of which one is presently aware. One would not suspect that the object of consciousness would change, and if it did change the new object would completely obliterate the previous one so that one would not be aware of the change; the new object would become the total world.

To say that a present perception is synthesized with expected perceptions implies that certain perceptions are taken to be impossible, and if an impossible perception in fact takes place, then the object of perception literally changes.[13] If, for example, the object of my consciousness is a chest of drawers, I take it that if I turn the chest around I will see a back panel, or, if there is none, the backs of the drawers.

The back of the chest is something I may never have seen, yet it forms part of the object of my consciousness. If I do turn the chest around and there is no back panel and no drawers, the object literally changes into something else — something like a stage prop. That there are limits to the possible perceptions associated with an object is a necessary aspect of consciousness. The structure of consciousness necessarily entails principles of coherence. What the principles are may change, but unless some principles are presupposed, objects of consciousness, and consequently consciousness itself, are impossible.[14] One might wonder whether such principles characterize the world independently of consciousness, but, to a phenomenologist like Husserl, such a question is subordinate to the temporal nature of objects of consciousness, and not the other way around.

Like the object of consciousness, the subject of consciousness is also necessarily temporal, for the subject identifies itself with the subject of previous and expected acts of consciousness at the same time that it distinguishes itself temporally from other such acts.[15] If the subject did not both identify itself with itself and also distinguish its various acts of consciousness temporally, all its various modes of consciousness (such as remembering, remembering that it remembered, perceiving, hoping, expecting) would come to the same thing. A consciousness in which there is no distinction between remembering, perceiving and expecting is one that excludes self-awareness, for self-awareness presupposes a contrast between self and other-than-self, and this contrast entails temporal distinctions and identifications that associate things that are temporally distinct.[16] A non-temporal consciousness, one may infer, also lacks freedom and responsibility, for planning and responding both fall away when expecting, hoping and remembering collapse into perceiving.

While various modes of consciousness must be distinguised and may be as contrasting and even as disparate as living toward the future and living from the past in Beethoven's Sonata, Op. 90/i, Husserl maintains that the subject will always identify itself with itself. I will not, for example, suddenly become the subject of someone else's perceptions, hopes or self-awareness. Principles of coherence characterize the subject of consciousness just as much as the object. Even though one's understanding of the principles may change, consciousness entails that the subject be in some sense coherent. Consequently, the structure of consciousness implies that even disparate modes of consciousness must be in some sense mutually reinforcing.

Heidegger is no less insistent than Husserl that both the subject and object of consciousness are temporal. The phenomenon of human existence requires temporality, although it is not the case that temporality in some sense exists before human existence happens (as if human beings somehow walked into a preexisting structure), nor that human existence creates it (as if human existence somehow preceded temporality so that it could create it). Human existence is always already temporal (and does not somehow become temporal, having previously been non-temporal), and temporality always already involves the consciousness of a subject in a world. But because he looks so much more sensitively than Husserl at particular modes of consciousness, Heidegger disagrees with his teacher over the subject's self-identification. Because Husserl believes that the subject of consciousness necessarily entails principles of coherence, it could not occur to him that the subject might fall into the world, lose itself and be fundamentally at odds with itself. Heidegger's assertion that for the most part the "who" of being-in-the-world (the subject of consciousness in Husserl's vocabulary) is the inauthentic self that lets itself be in the way in which "one is" has the advantage of resembling the way we in fact lead our lives. The complexity and irrationality entailed in allowing for contradiction within the subject of consciousness rings true to concrete experience, though it severely wounds our ideal images of ourselves.

The two disparate shapes simultaneously generated by Beethoven's Quartet, Op. 132/i, exemplify a way of experiencing the contrast between past, present and future that is as irreducibly complex as that analyzed by Heidegger. Beethoven's movement exemplifies the kind of process which allows the decisions of a free agent to have an effect, but in which there is a limit on the extent to which the agent can shape events to be so congruent with itself that it fully manifests itself through them. In the kind of temporal process exemplified by the end-directed shape of Op. 132/i, the self is free and responsbile for events. But in the middle-focused shape, the temporal process is to be undergone as much as it is to be directed, for the extent to which occurrences are in fact events that actualize the self by actualizing the goals of its past is fundamentally ambiguous. This ambiguity attenuates the degree to which the self can take moral responsibility for itself and its future.

Yet, because the end-directed shape is so unusual that it freshly confirms the process of a self moving from a past through a decision to actualization, the movement does not suggest that the self merely goes through the motions of trying to actualize itself. It is not as though this self, like the self in late Romanticism, expected to fail. It may have limits and may know that it cannot fully actualize itself; yet because, perhaps, it cannot know where those limits lie, it continues to behave as though total self-actualization were possible. The temporal process exemplified by Op. 132/i is such that the deciding agent is always surprised and dismayed when it fails, even though it knows well enough that it will never fully succeed. It is a temporality, like Heidegger's, in which one experiences the contrast between what is and what will be in two conflicting ways simultaneously.

Although Op. 132/i rejects Newtonian temporality and although it both affirms and rejects the temporality of Classic sonata-allegro form, it does not anticipate the kind of temporal process that is usually associated with Romanticism. For the temporal process in Op. 132/i does not resemble those kinds of temporality in which fulfillment takes place in some atemporal realm and in which consequently one would be foolish to see fulfillment in the temporal process and in which the self's alienation from its temporal actualization is its most profound expression. Rather, Op. 132/i is more like those kinds of temporality in which the self continues to be thoroughly temporal, and to be what it temporally experiences just as much when what it experiences is an occurrence that extends its past (rather than expressing the self) as when it concretely actualizes itself. In this way of experiencing the contrast between past, present and future, there is no hint that one ought to reject the temporal process in order to discover an inmost, radically non-public self. For in it, self-discovery — like self-expression, which has self-discovery as a goal — can evidently only be temporally deployed and must risk being fragmentary. The self must fact the shadowy, equivocal nature of the fulfillments it shapes and somehow see itself as the subject of the experiences it undergoes but cannot shape. Yet evidently it still may, and still does, persistently direct itself toward a future that will establish the goals for which it and its past have been struggling.

Notes

1. The assertion that these articulations are unusual is supported by the following data. Only 19% of the 1809–1814 bridges begin with fresh material following a decisive cadence. Only 16% have a weak caesura between the bridge and the second theme. All of the 1809–14 movements in the study from which these data are derived separate the exposition closing from the end of the second theme more distinctly than Beethoven does in Op. 90/i. Only 12% of the 1809–14 developments begin by continuing the cadential motif ending the exposition. Only 18% of the developments have no gestures separated by a cadence. Only 19% of the retransitions begin without an articulation and with no change of motif. None of the 1809–14 movements studied has a recapitulation that begins without some sort of harmonic change.

2. *The Beethoven Quartets*, p. 245.

3. See *ibid.*, p. 247.

4. See Rosen, *op. cit.*, p. 73.

5. *The Beethoven Quartets*, p. 245.

6. *Op. cit.*, p. 373.

7. *Ibid.*, p. 386.

8. *Ibid.*, pp. 320–22.

9. For a different treatment of the problem that Heidegger seems to suggest that human existence is at once authentic and inauthentic, see Joan Stambaugh, "An Inquiry into Authenticity and Inauthenticity in *Being and Time*" in John Sallis, ed., *Radical Phenomenology:Essays in Honor of Martin Heidegger* (1978), pp. 153–61. Interpreting *Being and Time* in light of Heidegger's later emphases, Stambaugh insists that because man is the place where Being takes place and because his relation to Being is what authenticates human existence, the authentic is its "fundamental level" (p. 160). Stambaugh seems to take inauthenticity much less seriously than *Being and Time* does. Like Husserl (and the philosophical tradition generally), she seems to presuppose that human existence must be more integral than *Being and Time* does, and consequently she does not feel any bite to the questions, why does man flee from the authentic and how does he come to relate himself to Being in spite of this flight?

10. English translation (1970), p. 33.

11. *Ibid.*, pp. 39–40.

12. *Ibid.*, p. 43.

13. *Ibid.*, pp. 44–45.

14. *Ibid.*, pp. 53–54.

15. *Ibid.*, p. 66.

16. *Ibid.*, p. 85.

Appendix:
A Sample of Sonata-Allegro Movements Published in Vienna, 1795–1826

I. 1795–1800

Muzio Clementi, Sonata in C for Piano (Violin or Flute, Cello), Op. 33/i.*
Muzio Clementi, Sonata in C for Piano, Op. 34/1/i.
Muzio Clementi, Sonata in G minor for Piano, Op. 34/2/i.
Muzio Clementi, Sonata in C for Piano (Violin, Cello), Op. 36/1/i.
Muzio Clementi, Sonata in G for Piano (Violin, Cello), Op. 36/2/i.
Anton Eberl, Sonata in C minor for Piano, Op. 1/i.
Josef Eybler, Trio in C for Violin, Viola, Cello, Op. ?/i.
Josef Eybler, Sonata in C minor for Piano (Violin), Op. ?/i.
Josef Eybler, Quartet in D, Op. 1/1/i.
Josef Eybler, Trio in E-flat for Piano, Violin, Cello, Op. 4/1/i.
G. Tepper de Ferguson, Piano Sonata in E-flat, Op. 2/i.
Em. Al. Förster, Sonata in G for Piano, Op. 12/1/i.
Em. Al. Förster, Sonata in D for Piano, Op. 12/2/i.
Em. Al. Förster, Sonata in E-flat for Piano, Op. 15/1/i.
Em. Al. Förster, Sonata in C minor for Piano, Op. 15/3/i.
Em. Al. Förster, Quartet in A, Op. 16/6/i.
Em. Al. Förster, Sonata in C for Piano, Op. 17/1/i.
Em. Al. Förster, Sonata in E-flat for Piano, Op. 17/2/i.
Ferdinand Fränzel, Quartet in C, Op. 2/1/i.
Ferdinand Fränzel, Quartet in G, Op. 2/2/i.
Ferdinand Fränzel, Quartet in A, Op. 2/3/i.
Abbé Gelinek, Trio in E-flat for Piano, Violin, Cello, Op. 10/i.
Adalbert Gyrowetz, Sonata in D for Piano (Violin, Cello), Op. 10/1/i.
Adalbert Gyrowetz, Sonata in G for Piano (Violin, Cello), Op. 18/1/i.
Adalbert Gyrowetz, Quartet in A, Op. 21/1/i.
Adalbert Gyrowetz, Sonata in G for Piano (Violin, Cello), Op. 28/2/i.
Adalbert Gyrowetz, Quartet in E-flat, Op. 29/1/i.

*Instruments in parentheses are called "accompanying" or "obbligato" instruments on the title page of the original edition.

Adalbert Gyrowetz, Quartet in G, Op. 29/2/i.
Leopold Koželuch, Sonata in B-flat for Piano (Violin, Cello), Op. 41/1/i.
Leopold Koželuch, Sonata in D for Piano (Violin, Cello), Op. 41/2/i.
G.F. Lickl, Sonata in C for Piano (Violin, Cello), Op. ?/1/i.
Jean Mederitsch, Trio in A minor for Violin, Violin, Cello, Op. 12/2/ı.
Ignaz Pleyel, Sonata in F for Piano (Violin, Cello), Op. 37/1/i.
Ignaz Pleyel, Sonata in C for Piano (Violin, Cello), Op. 37/2/i.
Ignaz Pleyel, Sonata in B-flat for Piano (Violin, Cello), Op. 41/1/i.
Ambros Rieder, Quartet in E-flat, Op. 8/1/i.
Ambros Rieder, Quartet in G, Op. 8/2/i.
Ambros Rieder, Quartet in C, Op. 8/3/i.
D. Steibelt, Quartet, in E-flat, Op. 8/1/i.
D. Steibelt, Quartet in C, Op. 8/2/i.
D. Steibelt, Quartet in F minor, Op. 8/3/i.
G.B. Viotti, Trio in A for 2 Violins, Cello, Op. 4/1/i.
G.B. Viotti, Trio in D minor for Violin, Violin, Cello, Op. 4/2/i.
G.B. Viotti, Trio in D for Violin, Violin, Cello, Op. 4/3/i.
G.B. Viotti, Duo in F minor for 2 Violins, Op. 5/4/iv.
G.B. Viotti, Duo in C for 2 Violins, Op. 5/5/i.
Joseph Wölfl, Sonata in C for Piano (Violin), Op. 2/1/i.
Joseph Wölfl, Sonata in G for Piano (Violin), Op. 2/2/i.
Joseph Wölfl, Quartet in F, Op. 5/2/i.
Joseph Wölfl, Quartet in C minor, Op. 5/3/i.

II. 1801–08

Gottlieb Bachmann, Quartet in C, Op. 7/1/i.
Leonard de Call, Serenade in C for Guitar, Violin, Viola, Cello, Op. 3/i.
Jean Charles Coló, Sonata in C for Piano, Op. 1/i.
J.B. Cramer, Sonata in D for Piano, Op. 36/i.
A. Diabelli, Sonata in F for Piano à 4, Op. 24/i.
Anton Eberl, Sonata in C for Piano, Op. 16/i.
Anton Eberl, Sonata in A for Piano, Cello, Op. 36/i.
Josef Eybler, Quintet in A for Violin, 2 Violas, Cello, Bass, Op. 6/2/i.
Josef Eybler, Sonata in C for Piano (Violin), Op. 9/1/i.
Em. Al. Förster, Quartet in C, Op. 21/1/i.
Abbé Gelinek, Sonata in F for Piano, Op. 24/i.
Adalbert Gyrowetz, Sonata in F for Piano (Violin, Cello), Op. 34/1/i.
Peter Haensel, Quartet in D, Op. 10/2/i.
Peter Haensel, Quartet in G, Op. 14/2/i.
Peter Haensel, Quartet in E minor, Op. 17/1/i.
Peter Haensel, Quartet in B, Op. 18/i.
Peter Haensel, Quartet in C, Op. 20/3/i
Johann Nepomuk Hummel, Sonata in E-flat for Piano, Op. 13/i.
Johann Nepomuk Hummel, Trio No. 2 in F for Piano, Violin, Cello, Op. 22/i.
Rudolf Kreutzer, Trio in A for 2 Violins, Cello, Op. ?/1/i.
Franz Krommer, Quartet in B-flat, Op. 19/3/i.
S. Molitor, Trio in D for Violin, Viola, Guitar, Op. 6/i.
Silvere Muller, Quartet in B-flat, Op. 3/2/i.

F.A. Pössinger, Quintet in F minor for 2 Violins, 2 Violas, Cello, Op. 3/2/i.
F.A. Pössinger, Duo in B minor for Violin, Viola, Op. 4/3/i.
F.A. Pössinger, Quartet in C minor, Op. 8/1/i.
F.A. Pössinger, Quartet in A, Op. 8/3/iv.
F.A. Pössinger, Quartet in D, Op. 18/2/i.
Felix Radicati, Quartet in C. Op. 14/1/i.
P.J. Rode, Quartet in F, Op. 12/i.
A. Rolla, Duo in G for 2 Violins, Op. ?/2/i.
A. Rolla, Duo in F minor for 2 Violins, Op. ?/i.
A. Rolla, Quartet in D minor, Op. 5/2/i.
A. Rolla, Quartet in E-flat, Op. 5/3/i.
A. Romberg, Quartet in E, Op. 7/2/i.
A. Romberg, Quartet in C, Op. 7/3/i.
A. Romberg, Quartet in C, Op. 7/3/iv.
A. Romberg, Quartet in A, Op. 11/i.
A. Romberg, Quartet in B-flat, Op. 16/3/ii.
A. Romberg, Trio in F for Violin, Viola, Cello, Op. 8/i.
Johann Schadek, Sonata in E minor for Piano, Op. ?/2/i.
Schweitzer, Trio in E-flat for 2 Violins, Cello, Op. 2/1/i.
Schweitzer, Trio in D for 2 Violins, Cello, Op. 2/2/i.
Johann Spech, Quartet in G minor, Op. 2/1/i.
Johann Spech, Quartet in G minor, Op. 2/1/iv.
Johann Spech, Quartet in E-flat, Op. 2/2/i.
Johann Spech, Quartet in E-flat, Op. 2/2/iv.
Johann Spech, Quartet in C, Op. 2/3/iv.
D. Steibelt, Sonata in E-flat for Piano, Op. ?/i.
F. Teyber, Sonata No. 1 in E-flat for Violin, Piano, Op. ?/i.
F. Teyber, Sonata No. 2 in B-flat for Violin, Piano, Op. ?/i.
F. Teyber, Sonata No. 3 in G for Violin, Piano, Op. ?/i
L. Tomasini, Quartet in A, Op. 8/1/i.
L. Tomasini, Quartet in D minor, Op. 8/2/i.
L. Tomasini, Quartet in B-flat, Op. 8/3/iv.
Benoit Tuttowitsch, Quartet in G minor, Op. 1/2/i.
B. Viguerie, Sonata in D for Piano, Op. ?/2/i.
J. Wanhal, Sonata in D for Violin, Piano, Op. ?/i.
J. Wanhal, Sonata No. 2 in B-flat for Piano, Op. ?/i.
J. Wanhal, Sonata No. 3 in F for Piano, Op. ?/i.
Anton Wranitzsky, Quartet in A minor, Op. 13/2/i.

III. 1809–14

J.X. Brauchle, Sonata in F for Piano, op. 5/i.
J.B. Cramer, Sonata in E-flat for Piano, Op. 41/i.
J.B. Cramer, Sonata in A minor for Piano, Op. 53/i.
Anton Diabelli, Sonata No. 3 in C for Piano à 4, Op. 37/i
Anton Diabelli, Sonata in B-flat for Piano à 4, Op. 38/i
Mauro Giuliani, Duo in A for Guitar, Violin, Op. ?/i.
Adalbert Gyrowetz, Sonata in A for Piano (Violin, Cello), Op. 60/2/i
Adalbert Gyrowetz, Sonata in D for Piano (Violin, Cello), Op. 60/3/i.

Peter Haensel, Quartet in F, Op. 22/2/i.
Peter Haensel, Duo in G for 2 Violins, Op. 23/1/i.
Peter Haensel, Duo in D for 2 Violins, Op. 23/2/i.
Peter Haensel, Duo in D minor for 2 Violins, Op. 24/1/i.
Peter Haensel, Duo in B-flat for 2 Violins, Op. 24/3/i.
Peter Haensel, Quintet in F for 2 Violins, 2 Violas, Cello, Op. 28/i.
Johann Nepomuk Hummel, Trio in G for Piano, Violin, Cello, Op. 35/i.
F.A. Kanne, Sonata in A for Piano, Op. 1/i.
Leopold Koželuch, Sonata in D minor for Piano, Op. 51/3/i.
Conradin Kreutzer, Quartet in E minor for Piano, Violin, Viola, Cello, Op. ?/i.
Franz Krommer, Quintet in E-flat for Flute, Violin, 2 Violas, Cello, Op. 66/i.
Franz Krommer, Quartet in F minor, Op. 68/1/i.
Franz Krommer, Quartet in C, Op. 68/2/i.
Franz Krommer, Quartet in G, Op. 74/2/i.
Franz Krommer, Quartet in D minor, Op. 73/3/i.
G. Lickl, Quartet in C for Oboe, Violin, Viola, Cello, Op. 26/1/i.
Josef Mayseder, Quartet in A, Op. 1/i.
Josef Mayseder, Quartet in A flat, Op. 7/i.
Ignaz Moscheles, Sonata in D for Piano, Op. 22/i.
Georg Onslow, Quartet in B-flat, Op. 4/1/i.
I.P. Pixis, Sonata in C minor for Piano, Op. 10/i.
Antoine Polzelli, Trio in E-flat for Clarinet, Viola, Cello, Op. 4/i.
Fred. Raiger, Sonata in B-flat for Piano, Violin, Op. 6/i.
Fred. Raiger, Trio in G for Flute, Violin, Cello, Op. 7/i.
Antonin Reicha, Trio in A minor for Violin, Viola, Cello, Op. ?/iv.
Ferd. Ries, Sonatina in F for Piano (Violin), Op. 30/3/i.
P.J. Riotte, Trio in E-flat for Piano, Violin, Cello, Op. 26/i.
P.J. Riotte, Trio in F for Piano, Violin, Cello, Op. 49/i.
Jean Spech, Sonata in F for Piano (Violin), Op. 12/i.
Johann Spech, Sonata in E-flat for Piano, Violin, Op. 16/1/i.
L. Spohr, Quartet in G minor, Op. 27/i.
Paul Struck, Quartet in F for Clarinet, Violin, Viola, Cello, Op. 12/i.
C.M. von Weber, Sonata in C for Piano, Op. 24/i.
Francois Weiss, Quartet in G, Op. 8/1/i.
Francois Weiss, Quartet in C minor, Op. 8/2/i.

IV. 1815–23

Ignatz Assmayer, Sonata in A for Piano (Violin), Op. 33/i.
Leonard von Call, Quartet in G, Op. 140/i.
Francesco de Contin, Quartet in E-flat, Op. 4/1/i.
F. Contin, Quartet in C, Op. 4/2/i
F. Contin, Quartet in B-flat, Op. 4/3/i.
F. Contin, Quartet in G, Op. 7/i.
Charles Czerny, Sonata in A minor for Piano, Op. 13/i.
Anton Diabelli, Sonata in D for Piano à 4, Op. 33/i.
Anton Diabelli, Sonata in G for Piano, Violin, Op. 47/i.
J.L. Dussek, Sonata in B-flat for Piano, Op. 35/i.
J.L. Dussek, Sonata in B-flat for Piano, Op. 40(/)/i.

F.E. Fesca, Quartet in E-flat, Op. 1/1/i.
F.E. Fesca, Quartet in B-flat, Op. 1/3/i.
F.E. Fesca, Quartet in B minor, Op. 2/1/i.
F.E. Fesca, Quartet in G minor, Op. 2/2/i.
F.E. Fesca, Quartet in D, Op. 3/2/i.
F.E. Fesca, Quartet in C minor, Op. 4/i.
F.E. Fesca, Sinfonie in E-flat, Op. 6/i.
John Field, Sonata in A for Piano, Op. ?/i.
Mauro Giuliani, Grand Duo in A for Guitar, Violin (or Flute), Op. 85/i.
Peter Haensel, Quartet in D, Op. 33/i.
Anton Halm, Quartet in D, Op. 38/i.
George Hellmesberger, Quartet in D, Op. 1/i.
Joseph Hoffmann, Quintet in F for 2 Violins, 2 Violas, Cello, Op. ?/ii.
Johann Nepomuk Hummel, Sonata in D for Piano (Violin), Op. 50/i.
Johann Nepomuk Hummel, Septet in D minor for Piano, Flute, Oboe, Horn, Viola,
    Cello, Bass, Op. 74/i.
Johann Nepomuk Hummel, Quintet in E-flat minor for Piano, Violin, Viola, Cello,
    Bass, Op. 87/i.
Franz Krommer, Trio in F for Violin, Viola, Cello, Op. 96/i.
Edouard Baron de Lannoy, Sonata in A for Piano (Violin), Op. 6/i.
M.J. Leidesdorf, Quartet in F for Piano, Violin, Viola, Cello, Op. 123/i.
Joseph Mayseder, Sonata in E flat for Piano, Violin, Op. ?/i,
Joseph Mayseder, Duo in G for 2 Violins, Op. 30/1/i.
Ignace Moscheles, Duo in B-flat for Piano, Cello, Op. 34/i.
Ignace Moscheles, Sonata in E for Piano, Op. 41/i.
Georg Onslow, Quartet in G, Op. 10/1/i.
Georg Onslow, Trio in E minor for Piano, Violin, Cello, Op. 14/1/i.
Georg Onslow, Trio in E-flat for Piano, Violin, Cello, Op. 14/2/i.
Georg Onslow, Sonata in C minor for Piano, Cello, Op. 16/2/i.
Ferdinand Ries, Trio in E for Piano, Violin, Cello, Op. 2/i.
Carlo Godfredo Salzman, Quartet in F, Op. ?/i.
L. Spohr, Quartet in E-flat, Op. 29/1/i.
L. Spohr, Quartet in E-flat, Op. 29/l/iv.
L. Spohr, Quartet in C, Op. 29/2/i.
L. Spohr, Quartet in C, Op. 29/2/iv.
L. Spohr, Quartet in F minor, Op. 29/3/i.
L. Spohr, Quartet in F minor, Op. 29/3/iv.
L. Spohr, Quartet in A, Op. 30/i.
L. Spohr, Nonet in F for Violin, Viola, Cello, Bass, Flute, Oboe, Clarinet, Bassoon, ,
    Horn, Op. 31/i.
L. Spohr, Nonet in F for Violin, Viola, Cello, Bass, Flute, Oboe, Clarinet, Bassoon, ,
    Horn, Op. 31/iv.
L. Spohr, Octet in E for Violin, 2 Violas, Cello, Bass, Clarinet, 2 Horns, Op. 32/i.
L. Spohr, Quintet in E-flat for 2 Violins, 2 Violas, Cello, Op. 33/6/i.
L. Spohr, Quintet in E-flat for 2 Violins, 2 Violas, Cello, Op. 33/6/iv.
Benoit Urban, Sonata in G for Piano, Violin, Cello, Op. ?/i.
Charles Angelus Winkhler, Trio in E minor for Piano, Flute, Viola, Op. 15/i.
J.H. Worzischek, Sonata in G for Piano, Violin, Op. 5/i.

V. 1824–26

Leopoldine Blahetka, Trio in D minor for Piano, Violin, Cello, Op. 5/1.
Leopold Eustachl Czapek, Duo in F minor for Piano, Violin, Op. 24/i.
Charles Czerny, Sonata sentimentale in G for Piano à 4, Violin, Cello, Op. 120/i.
F.E. Fesca, Quartet in D, Op. 34/i.
F. Grutsch, Duo in F for 2 Violins, Op. 7/1/i.
F. Grutsch, Duo in A for 2 Violins, Op. 7/2/i.
F. Grutsch, Duo in D minor for 2 Violins, Op. 7/3/i.
J.N. Hummel, Trio in E-flat for Piano, Violin, Cello, Op. 93/i.
J.N. Hummel, Sonata in D for Piano, Op. 106/i.
Fred Kalbrenner, Duo in F for Harp, Piano, Op. 82/i.
Conradin Kreutzer, Quintet in E-flat for 2 Violins, 2 Violas, Cello, Op. 62/i.
Franz Lechner, Sonata in F-sharp minor for Piano, Op. ?/i.
Franz Lechner, Sonata in A for Piano, Cello, Op. 14/i.
Leon St. Lubin, Quartet in D minor, Op. 19/i.
Leon St. Lubin, Quartet in D minor, Op. 19/iv.
Joseph Mayseder, Trio in B-flat for Piano, Violin, Cello, Op. 34/i.
Joseph Mayseder, Sonata in D for Piano, Violin, Op. 40/i.
Joseph Mayseder, Sonata in E minor for Piano, Violin, Op. 42/i.
Georg Onslow, Sonata in F minor for Piano à 4, Op. 22/i.
Georg Onslow, Quintet in E-flat, Op. 23/i.
Joseph Panny, Quintet No. 2 in F, Op. 19/2/i.
Jerome Payer, Sonata in C for Piano à 4, Op. 89/i.
F.A. Pössinger, Duo in C for Violins, Op. 38/1/i.
F.A. Pössinger, Duo in D for 2 Violins, Op. 38/2/i.
F.A. Pössinger, Duo in E minor for 2 Violins, Op. 38/3/i.
Carl Gottfried Salzmann, Sonata in F for Piano, Op. ?/i.
Carl Gottfried Salzmann, Sonata in A for Piano, Op. ?/i.
J.C. Louis Wolf, Sonata in C minor for Piano, Violin, Op. 2.
J.H. Worzischek, Sonata in B-flat minor for Piano, Op. 20/i.

Subject Index